Holy Living

THE MINDSET OF JESUS

By Herbert Luhn

CREST BOOKS
The Salvation Army National Publications
Alexandria, VA

Published by Crest Books
The Salvation Army National Headquarters
615 Slaters Lane
Alexandria, VA 22313
Phone: 703/684-5523
Fax: 703/302-8617

Major Allen Satterlee, Editor in Chief and National Literary Secretary
Judith L. Brown, Crest Books Manager
Roger Selvage, Art Director
Henry Cao, Cover Design

Available from The Salvation Army Supplies and Purchasing Departments

Des Plaines, IL – (847) 937-8896
West Nyack, NY – (888) 488-4882
Atlanta, GA – (800) 786-7372
Long Beach, CA – (847) 937-8896

Printed in the United States of America

ISBN: 978-0-9831482-7-2

Library of Congress Cataloging-in-Publication Data

Luhn, Herbert.
Holy living : the mindset of Jesus / by Herbert Luhn.
pages cm
Includes bibliographical references and index.
ISBN 978-0-9831482-7-2 (alk. paper)
1. Holiness. I. Title.
BT767.L84 2013
248.4--dc23

2012047593

The cover image, "Metamorphosis," was made available from the Journeys with the Messiah collection of fine art photographs depicting the messages of Jesus.

Using his unique story-telling skills, award-winning fashion photographer Michael Belk embarked on a journey to share the modern-day relevance and significance of Jesus. The result is a beautiful and compelling collection of fine art images—like no other—featuring a first century Jesus interacting with modern day people like you and me.

Produced in the ancient city of Matera, Italy, this one-of-a-kind photographic journey incites and inspires a fresh perspective of Jesus. All 45 images of the Journeys with the Messiah collection can be viewed and purchased at www.TheJourneysProject.com.

Journeys with the Messiah. Feeding a world hungry to hear God's voice while feeding the hungry.

Preface

For a long time I have felt the need for a book that would provide a road map to a holy life. Perhaps this has been because of the difficulty I have had finding the way. Permit me to sketch the troubled path I followed.

I was saved at a youth rally at the age of 12 and began attending The Salvation Army in my home town of Racine, Wisconsin. I took an active part in the corps during my teen-age years, and I was among soldiers from my corps and other churches who attended an annual holiness campaign. Stimulated by this religious teaching and the testimony of others, I yearned for an experience that would put an end to the struggle with self and sin.

I hungered for the holiness experience. I was taught that once I was fully sanctified and filled with the Holy Spirit, my natural selfishness would be replaced by an overwhelming love, and my struggles with my carnal nature would be over. Further I was advised that, after being saved, the carnal nature, like the roots of a tree, not only had to come out but would be removed in a divine process of eradication at the moment of entire sanctification—a second work of grace. My part was to make a full consecration of my life to God, and to trust him. God's part was to sanctify me and work this miracle in me. If it didn't happen right away, I should wait. God would eventually come with a baptism of the Holy Spirit and replace the carnal nature with a perfect love.

But for me, it never happened. Many times of sincere seeking, resulted in repeated disappointment. I can recall times of crisis-praying, crying out to God to sanctify me. I would claim it by faith, often experiencing seasons of euphoria in which I tried to convince myself it had happened. But I discovered that the old roots were still very much there! In spite of these spiritual highs, I seemed to be constantly thwarted by the overwhelming and unrelenting reality of a self-seeking human nature. I was a consecrated follower of Jesus Christ with a human nature prone to sin.

My spiritual advisors had all sorts of explanations. "The roots are gone," they said, "and now instead of temptations coming from within they are coming from without, that is, Satan attacking me." I was told to be patient; the overwhelming power of love would come to me. Or perhaps my consecration was not complete. But these explanations seemed like word games that dodged the real issue.

I discovered that I was not alone. Many expressed to me the same confusion regarding holiness teaching and doctrine. Others told me that they had simply given up, concluding that a holy life was not for them. They too wanted a clear roadmap.

This book represents my effort to provide such a road map. While it is not autobiographical, it is the result of insights the Lord has given me in the years of my seeking. A "eureka" moment came with the revelation that in the mindset of Jesus was the key to living a holy life. In the 40 years since then I have enjoyed a holy walk with my Lord.

I write simply. This is not a theological treatise, but a handbook for seekers. It contains discussion questions at the end of each chapter that could be used in Bible Study groups. A Study Guide has been provided as an Appendix.

The Apostle Paul, in writing to his protégé Timothy, said, "Beyond all question, the mystery of godliness is great" (1 Tim. 3:16). My prayer is that this book might help you as you face this mystery.

(All scripture verses quoted in this book are from the New International Version, unless otherwise noted.)

Acknowledgements

My profound appreciation goes to all who have encouraged and counseled me in the preparation of this manuscript. My wife has been my chief helper and encourager, sharing her skills in proofreading and offering her sanctified common-sense advice. Other family members have helped immensely in the endless task of writing and re-writing. I must mention also that many of my close colleagues, fellow officers in The Salvation Army, have helped me navigate through the theological minefield a study such as this must traverse. Special thanks also go to Caleb Sjogren and Lt. Colonel Marlene Chase, who have given invaluable assistance in final editing. Above all, there has been the driving influence and help of the Holy Spirit who has urged me on to the completion of this project

Contents

Chapter 1

The Starting Point

"Pastor Molests Children," the headlines scream. "Church Official Embezzles Offerings," says another. Sadly, such instances of carnal behavior by Christians are trumpeted in the secular press. We who are part of the body of Christ cringe. In a recent survey it was found that one of the reasons many give for not attending church is that so many hypocrites can be found there. While we admit that many of those who go to church are not perfect, we must also admit that a great lack of holy living exists among believers.

This poor behavior problem is compounded by the fact that confusion exists today about what is right and what is wrong. A fog of moral uncertainty has engulfed our secular age. The ancient guideposts are no longer visible. Believing that no absolute truth exists, many seekers wander without a compass.

In spite of this malaise, many earnest Christians aspire to live a holy life. The good news is that above the fog, the sun still shines. The eternal God, the Creator/Ruler of the universe, has not changed. He still longs to see holy living in his followers, living with high moral and ethical standards.

The starting point for those who aspire to live a holy life is the holiness of God. The greater our awareness of his holiness, the greater will be our hope of becoming holy ourselves. So let's start at the beginning by taking a close look at God.

The very essence of God is holiness. He is purity and moral perfection. His holiness is the fountainhead from which his attributes of love, truth, justice, faithfulness, and grace flow. The one adjective that wraps up all other words that might be used to describe God is the word "holy."

> What if God stopped loving? He would no longer be holy.
>
> What if God began to lie? He would no longer be holy.
>
> What if God treated people unfairly? He would no longer be holy.
>
> What if God became indifferent to His creation? He would no longer be holy.
>
> What if God no longer kept His promises? He would no longer be holy.
>
> What if God withdrew His grace? He would no longer be holy.

"Holy" gets right to the heart of the revelation of God as found in the Bible. He is repeatedly called "the Holy One of Israel" (Ps.89:18, Isa. 1:4, Jer. 50:29). This is not some minor theme, some marginal idea that can be lightly set aside. Here instead is the very pulse of heaven, "Holy, Holy, Holy." God's holiness radiates in the Old Testament like the light reflecting from the thousand facets of a large diamond.

> "Those who are able to study the Bible in its original languages tell us that the root words which we translate 'holy,' 'holiness,' 'sanctify,' and 'sanctification' appear 700 times in the Old Testament and 400 times in the New Testament." (Bramwell Tripp)

God has made himself known as the holy God. This title distinguishes him from the pantheon of lesser supposed deities whose actions and desires are anything but holy. He makes this clear in the Bible:

> "Speak to the entire assembly of Israel and say to them: 'Be ye holy, because I, the Lord your God, am holy'" (Lev. 19:2).
>
> "I am the Lord, your Holy One, Israel's creator, your king" (Isa. 43:15).
>
> "Glory in his holy name, let the hearts of those who seek the Lord rejoice" (1 Chron. 16:10).

This is the starting point in our quest for human holiness--the realization that God is holy. It is the awareness of his holiness and the fact that we are created in his image that provides the ideal, the motivation, and the hunger to be holy. To recognize his holiness, and to stand in awe before him, must precede any effort to be holy. We will never reflect his holy image if our perception of God is less. Any concept of God that falls short of sensing his utter holiness is flawed and will hamper the search for holiness. Our God is a Holy God.

Biblical Heroes of Holiness

Isaiah was one who saw the holiness of God. In a vision at a time of political turmoil (King Uzziah had just died, Isaiah 6:1-8), he heard the seraphim in heaven singing "Holy, holy, holy." Seeing the holiness of God distressed him because of his own un-holiness. This vision sealed his desire to be holy like God. God was pleased with Isaiah's desire. He touched him, forgave his sins, and sent him on a life-long mission as his spokesperson.

Moses is another example of biblical holiness. He was humbled when he came into God's presence (Exodus 3:1-12). God spoke to him from a burning bush saying, "Moses, take off your shoes, for you are standing on holy ground." Moses was filled with awe. "Who am I that I should go. . . ?" But, he too, responded to this revelation of holiness with submissive obedience and began a forty-year epic journey that freed the children of Israel from slavery and brought them to their promised land.

On the way to Damascus, Saul of Tarsus was blinded by a vision. After he was delivered from this blindness, he became obedient to his heavenly vision. This vision of God (his holiness?) launched Saul as Paul into a power-packed preaching and teaching odyssey that helped shape the character and scope of the Christian Church for all time.

Other Saints

How many others like Moses, Isaiah and Paul have been thrust into larger-than-life missions because they saw the holiness of God? Every era has been blessed by those who have served God with a deep personal awareness of his holiness, and a burning desire to be filled with his Holy Spirit. We could write of Samuel Logan Brengle, who became The Salvation Army's Apostle of Holiness, or J. Hudson Taylor, the pioneer missionary to the interior of China, or John Wesley, the tireless teacher who started hundreds of classes focused on perfect love. And there have been literally thousands of other outstanding spiritual giants who were inspired by God's holiness.

In addition to these larger-than-life heroes, millions of others have lived quiet lives of holiness. They have cared for the sick, fed and clothed the poor, comforted the troubled, taught the children, and loved wherever God has placed them. It is these unnamed saints who have brought the essence of godliness into their cultures, and into our world at large. Oh that there were millions more!

Where do such people come from? While their backgrounds may vary, and the process of their development may differ, all were moved with a longing to please God. Their sense of his love and holiness resonated with their own inner feelings. They sought to match his holiness in their lives. Man dares the impossible and strives for the highest when he is convinced of the magnificent holiness of God.

Perhaps this is why God says so clearly, "Be holy because I, the Lord your God, am holy" (Lev. 19:2). We hear his challenge, and feel our own aspirations. Now dare we believe it is possible? If so, please press on.

Discussion Starters:

1. What thoughts come to your mind when you hear the word "holy?"
2. Discuss these scripture verses that also refer to the holiness of God: Psalms 145:17 I Chronicles 16:29
3. Which of these statements is more correct? Discuss why. God has holiness. God is holy.
4. The word "holy" in the Old Testament often means "sacred" or "set apart." Are there instances where the word also refers to moral purity (righteousness)? Note these verses: Deuteronomy 32:4 Hosea 14:9
5. Why would belief in the holiness of God help a person's spiritual life?
6. Tell of any person you have known who has lived a quiet life of holiness.

Chapter 2

Humankind at Its Best

One of the great unsolved mysteries of our world is the origin of humankind. Archeologists claim to have found human remains going back millenniums. While evolutionists claim development through natural selection, they have no convincing explanation for our unique abilities to speak, plan, and create. While the DNA of a human is very similar to that of the animal world, it is obvious that something must have happened along the way to make us extremely different, with mental and spiritual attributes unknown anywhere else in the physical universe.

This phenomenal difference is credited in the Bible to a special act of creation by God. It states that he created man and breathed into him and made him a living soul. He was made in God's own image, a thinking, speaking, and social being. While the Genesis record may seem to have a poetic-legend quality, it nevertheless resonates with us. We identify with its concepts. It has the ring of truth and authenticity to us. For this reason, we turn to the Bible to gain the insights we need to find the holiness we are seeking.

Humankind Created

The creation of Adam and Eve is presented as an instantaneous act. God brought them into existence and, as He had done after his other acts of creation, He felt good about it.

"God saw all that he had made, and it was very good (Genesis 1:31).

God had a right to take satisfaction in these first humans. What a wonder they were; the miraculous fusion of body, brain, and spirit, with systems to make them function properly. Here were creatures who, like God, could think, plan, love, appreciate, create and choose. Indeed, God created them in his own image.

"Then God said, 'Let us make man in our image, in our likeness' . . . So God created man in his own image, in the image of God he created him, male and female he created them" (Genesis 1:26, 27).

The holy God had made two living beings capable of reflecting his holiness. They were innocent, unstained by sin. Here was humankind at his best. We can only speculate as to what that meant for Adam and Eve. They were given the tasks of caring for the garden, naming the animals and reproducing and ruling over the earth (Genesis 2:15,19).

"God blessed them and said to them, 'Be fruitful and increase in number; fill the earth and subdue it. Rule over the fish of the sea and the birds of the air and over every living creature that moves on the ground'" (Genesis 1:28).

The Bible reveals very little about their early experiences in the garden, or how long they enjoyed this idyllic time. The fact that Adam and Eve were there with God suggests a period of fellowship, creatures with creator. It must have taken time for them to name all of the animals. Some speculate that God created such a being so as to have someone with whom to fellowship. If this is so, this fellowship must have been much appreciated by both parties.

Let's take a closer look at this first man, Adam. He was a flesh and blood human being, like us. God made him from dust.

"And the Lord God formed man of the dust of the ground, and breathed into his nostrils the breath of life; and man became a living soul" (Genesis 2:7 KJV).

Like the animals before him, Adam was designed to live on the earth. God gave him a mortal body with an immortal soul. Understanding the original constitution of man is very important to our search for holiness. Adam had a human body with all its natural instincts, yet he was at home with a holy God. Nothing in him was offensive to God's holiness. This is a foreshadowing of the relationship possible to all.

Let's consider the natural instincts given by God to Adam and Eve. First of all they had a natural inclination to relate to God. You might call this a spiritual instinct. Their desire was to please God, to worship and obey him. It was an awareness of God's sovereignty and their own humble status. It was recognition of their dependence upon him. This spiritual instinct still permeates the human race. It is seen in the varied expressions of worship that have been a part of all cultures through all time. It is also the inner longing behind our *own* desires to know God and to be holy like him. This spiritual instinct is what some have called a God-shaped vacuum in us that can only be satisfied by his presence. It is the initial working of the Holy Spirit in each human being, calling him back to God.

In addition to the spiritual instinct, they were given three dominant physical instincts. They were the same basic instincts as those given to all other living things, instincts necessary for survival. These instincts included the desires to eat, rest, and reproduce. These desires were part of being a physical being. They are not evil, but God's gracious endowments intended for their enjoyment and survival. These instincts or human drives are amoral in nature, and existed in Adam and Eve as they fellowshipped with a holy God. It is important to understand this, for we tend to demonize these drives, looking upon them as evil. These human attributes are not the enemy of holiness and must be accepted as the beautiful things they are. Coming to a right relationship with and understanding of these desires is an essential part of living a holy life.

Let's think a little more about these physical instincts, those normal to Adam and Eve in their primal condition. Their human bodies were endowed with desires that would assure their physical survival. Adam and Eve were subject to their pull. Disobeying God and yielding to these instincts led to their fall.

The Biblical account of their Fall and the temptations of Jesus help us identify these physical instincts.

"When the woman saw that the fruit of the tree was good for food and pleasant to the eye, and also desirable for gaining wisdom, she took some and ate it" (Genesis 3:6).

First, Eve was tempted to eat the forbidden fruit. She saw that it was good for food. Eating brought pleasure. She wanted to taste this appetizing fruit even though it meant disobeying God. Jesus' first temptation in the wilderness was to eat. The desire to bring satisfaction to the body is a universal instinct.

Next, we are told that the fruit was pleasing to her sight. Here we are introduced to the desire to acquire things. What the eye sees it wants to possess. The second temptation of Jesus also appealed to the eye. He was shown all the kingdoms of the world. This instinct is so strong that it often drives one to steal.

The third instinct seen here is a longing for status. Eve was told that eating the fruit would make her wise like God. Her position would be enhanced. Though the third temptation of Jesus was to test God by jumping from the temple, the public locale of this temptation, suggested it would bring approval and enhance his status with the people.

For the sake of simplicity, and taking somewhat of a leap here which will be explained later, let's just say that Adam's and Eve's three fundamental physical instincts were for Pleasure,

Possessions, and Position. Think of it! Here is a man in fellowship with God while possessing God-given instincts. It is obvious that these desires were not immoral. They were not the result of the Fall, having pre-existed the temptation. Humankind at its best were human beings, made in the image of God, endowed with spiritual desires in order to know and worship their creator and physical desires designed to assure their earthly survival.

Their order of importance was clearly established. They were to keep the spiritual first and put obedience to God ahead of all other desires. Their human drives were to be kept subservient to their spiritual relationship with God. This was the divinely established order: keep the spiritual first and other desires second. God warned them that if they reversed this order, and put their physical desires first, they would die.

In the next chapter we will examine the impact of Adam's and Eve's decision to ignore this proper order. They disobeyed God, and were shut out from their fellowship with God. They lost their close relationship with him. They died spiritually. As a result, all of their descendants inherit the same condition. Humankind was no longer innocent, but he would never be able to erase from its collective memory this time of bliss, this walk with a holy God. This memory continues today in all of us, prompting us to try to regain our holy status.

Discussion Starters:

1. If you had created man, would you have done anything differently?
2. Were Adam and Eve holy before the Fall?
3. In what ways were Adam and Eve made in God's image?
4. What *spiritual* instincts did Adam have?

5. What *physical* instincts did Adam have?

6. In what sense are the natural physical drives of hunankind amoral?

Chapter 3

Man's Infamous Choice and God's Response

Sometimes insignificant choices have massive consequences. A young man chose to dive into shallow water. His broken back made him an invalid for life. Two teenagers' lives were vastly altered when they made a poor choice leading to an unwanted pregnancy. The choice Adam and Eve made in the garden was like that, a simple yielding that brought monumental consequences.

As we consider our longing and hope for a holy life, it is important to observe just what happened at the Fall, for in a sense, the battle lines for gaining holiness were drawn there.

God had commanded Adam and Eve not to eat the fruit of one tree.

"And the Lord God commanded the man, 'You are free to eat from any tree in the garden, but you must not eat from the tree of the knowledge of good and evil, for when you eat of it you will surely die'" (Gen. 2:16).

We cannot know what they thought of this restriction. Though they were without sin, innocent before God, they were free to choose. They were vulnerable to temptation. Perhaps they longed just to do their own thing, to test the waters. Undoubtedly, the enemy was influencing their thinking. By the time they got to the tree, they were primed for making the wrong decision.

Satan, in the form of a serpent, made his bold move. He appeared and spoke to them.

"You will not surely die, the serpent said to the woman. For God knows that when you eat of it your eyes will be opened, and you will be like God, knowing good and evil" (Genesis 3:4).

His words must have weakened their resolve. Satan suggested that God was not being fair or honest with them, and that taking the forbidden fruit would bring great benefit to them. Here was the sinless couple under attack. They had an enemy who sought their harm.

In addition to an enemy, however, another very important factor influenced their decision. It was their natural instincts. Notice how these are revealed in Eve's reaction.

"When the woman saw that the fruit of the tree was good for food and pleasing to the eye and also desirable for gaining wisdom, she took some and ate it. She also gave some to her husband who was with her and he ate it" (Gen. 3:6).

Three natural instincts were active in Eve, instincts which reveal the dominant drives of the human nature. They are the hunger for Pleasure, Possessions, and Position. Eve saw the fruit as something good to eat, a means of *pleasure.* It was also seen as "pleasant to the eye," something to have as one's own, to *possess.* Here also was something to make one wise and like God, an appeal to her sense of *position.*

A Universal Pattern

Eve is not alone in her desires for Pleasure, Possessions, and Position. These pre-Fall desires permeate the human race. They are part of being a physical human being. The struggle with them is classic. The universal temptation is to yield to these desires even at the cost of disobeying God. It is the struggle between the immortal soul which desires to serve and obey God, and the mortal human body which craves the things of this world.

Centuries later, the Apostle John described the struggle in similar terms.

"Do not love the world or anything in the world. If anyone loves the world, the love of the Father is not in him. For everything in the world—the cravings of sinful man, the lust of his eyes, and the boasting of what he has and does, comes not from the Father but from the world" (1 John 2:15,16).

John identified three sins (temptations), "the cravings of sinful man," (Pleasure), "the lust of his eyes," (Possessions), and the "boasting of what he has and does," (Position). He recognized the common pathways of temptation in human nature. He infers that those who love them more than God belong to the world and are separated from God.

When Satan tempted Jesus in the wilderness at the beginning of his ministry, he appealed to these same three instincts. That Satan should so tempt him not only reveals how human Jesus was, but also helps to identify the natural human instincts found even in Jesus. But, unlike Adam and Eve, Jesus did not yield. He was fully committed to keeping the spiritual over the physical.

Charles Swindoll categorizes these desires in a similar way.

"Temptations come packaged in various shapes, sizes and colors . . . but most of them fall into one of three categories:

1. Material Temptation. This is lust for things. The things may be as large as a house or as small as a ring, as bright and dazzling as a new sports car or as dull and dusty as a two-hundred-year-old antique dresser.

2. Personal Temptation. This is lust for status—special recognition, the status of fame, fortune, power or authority. Having a title that makes heads turn, like 'top executive' or 'president or 'executive director' or even 'doctor.'
3. Sensual Temptation. This is lust for another person, the desire to have and enjoy the body of an individual, even though such pleasure is illegal and/or immoral" (*Man To Man*, Zondervan, p 96).

Separated From God

Adam and Eve disobeyed God, yielding to their human desires. They took and ate the forbidden fruit. They sinned. This deliberate choice of the physical over the spiritual had an immediate and profound impact on them. By their deed they became sinners. Their relationship with God was fractured. They felt alienated from him.

"Then the eyes of both of them were opened and they realized they were naked . . . and they hid from the Lord God among the trees of the garden" (Gen. 3:7-8).

In an instant, their innocence was gone. Guilt and fear replaced their peace. What had happened to bring about such a change? God had warned they would die if they ate of the tree. Obviously they had not died physically. What died was their relationship with God. Death means separation. They felt this separation inwardly even before they were expelled from the garden and from God's presence. It was as if God had said, "Well, if this is what you really want, I set you free. I give you over to live for your instinctive desires." The Psalmist says that God gave them over.

"But my people would not listen to me; Israel would not submit to me. So I gave them over to their stubborn hearts . . . To follow their own devices" (Psalm 81:11-12).

The Apostle Paul used the same term in describing those who knew God but did not glorify him.

"For although they knew God, they neither glorified him as God nor gave thanks to him . . . Therefore God gave them over in the sinful desires of their hearts" (Romans 1:21, 24).

Being given over by God meant that Adam and Eve would now be alone as they struggled to control their natural instincts.

A Lost Presence

For Adam and Eve, it was as if the lights had gone out in their soul. Sin and death had come upon them.

"Therefore, just as sin entered the world through one man, and death through sin . . ." (Romans 5:12).

These two, so blessed in knowing God, were suddenly separated from him. Their natural human desires were no longer restrained by his presence. Their natural desires for Pleasure, Possessions, and Position, drives given as a blessing for their survival and enjoyment, became depraved, turning into lust, greed and pride. Their human nature became a carnal nature, a strong disposition to sin. They were now sinners, far from the holy life God had intended for them.

It is impossible to over-emphasize the significance of the broken relationship with God. Humankind at its best is to be overshadowed by God's presence, in close relation with him, his Spirit within. Adam and Eve had this in the garden. God completed the essence of their existence. But with the loss of his presence, humankind became something less than the noble human beings God had created. Just as a brightly illuminated cloud turns a dark gray when the sun no longer shines on it, Adam and Eve lost their radiance when God withdrew from them. Their basic human desires, now no longer restrained by God's presence, became *the dominant drives of their lives.* These drives, when unrestrained, would lead to all sorts of sin and misery. Man was not just a sinner, he was impoverished of God, devoid of that part of himself that had brought beauty and meaning to his life

All Affected

This impoverishment was passed on. Adam and Eve's descendants would inherit their fallen nature. The spiritual death that had come upon them would be passed on to all who followed.

"... Sin entered the world through one man, and death through sin, and in this way death came to all men" (Romans 5:12).

Though it is hard to understand the Fall, it is not hard to recognize its reality. We see in ourselves the strong selfish tendency to lust, greed, and pride. Our natural drives tend to dominate our lives. If we were to honestly identify the things that are most important to us in our value system, money, sex, and power would be right up there. This is our natural disposition as the result of the Fall. Our value system is upside-down, opposite of what God intended, with physical gratification more important to us than spiritual things.

"They exchanged the truth of God for a lie, and worshipped and served created things rather than the Creator" (Romans 1:25).

Is it any wonder that today evil should be so prevalent and holiness so rare? All of mankind is dominated by inner drives that are inherently selfish. Those natural instincts, given to us for survival (drives for Pleasure, Possession, and Position), rule within the unregenerate human family, constrained only by cultural norms and laws. The result is chaos, suffering, frustration and unhappiness. A modern writer tells us this, too.

"The ceaseless search for happiness in possessions, indulgences, independence and self expression, which seems to characterize people of all ages, results in frustration, not life" (*Words of Life*, 1998).

If the collective temperature of the human race could be taken, it would be found to be feverish. The sinful infection of selfishness is rampant throughout the human family. It makes one wonder, "Is there a cure? Can man be healed of this infection, restored to spiritual health, and moved on to holiness of heart and life?" Yes, God has made a way. Man can be saved, and by God's grace, move on to become holy like his Creator.

We still have the freedom to choose. The Fall was a result of a poor choice, an act of the will, by which man set a higher value on earthly things than the things of God.

This freedom of choice provides an important foundation to our understanding of holiness as a Christ-centered mindset.

God's Response

The Fall of Adam and Eve did not take God by surprise, nor did it cause him to go back to the drawing board in his plans for humankind. Within his eternal, timeless realm, and before the creation of the world, God had a plan. This plan included a time of earthly existence, followed after death by an eternal spiritual existence. It also included a means of forgiveness and reconciliation with God, and the opportunity for men and women to become holy. They were to enjoy the goodness of God in a holy earthly life, and eventually step out of the vestibule of earthly life (in a mortal body), into the living room of a heavenly existence (in an immortal body). In both he would be holy, suited to live with God.

God's eternal plan was only slowly revealed. The Bible is our best source for understanding this plan. Gradually, through revelations to the patriarchs, the prophets and in historical events, the plan was unfolded. Jesus added immensely to the revelation.

Even though slowly revealed, the Bible tells us that this plan was completed in the mind of God before creation.

"We speak the wisdom of God in a mystery, even the hidden wisdom of God, which God ordained before the world unto our glory" (1 Cor. 2:7 KJV).

"For he chose us in him before the creation of the world to be holy and blameless in his sight" (Ephesians 1:4).

During his incarnation, Jesus spoke much of God's eternal plan for humankind, referring to it as the Kingdom of Heaven. He said this kingdom would have its start in us during our earthly life. People could become citizens of this kingdom by receiving Christ as their Savior, and Lord. This kingdom would have a profound effect on the present world. Its citizens, serving in love as salt and light, would introduce the love of God wherever they lived. Afterward, this earthy existence would continue in a spiritual realm.

"Jesus said, 'My kingdom is not of this world. If it were, my servants would fight to prevent my arrest by the Jews. But now my kingdom is from another place'" (John 18:36).

"In my Father's house are many rooms. I am going there to prepare a place for you. And if I go and prepare a place for you, I will come back and take you to be with me" (John 14:2-3).

The Apostle Paul, living in a time of persecution, had a very definite awareness of this eternal dimension. He clearly saw that human life was a pilgrimage through an alien land on the way toward receiving a great inheritance.

"I declare to you, brothers, that flesh and blood cannot inherit the kingdom of God . . . for the perishable must clothe itself with the imperishable, and the mortal with immortality" (1 Cor. 15:50, 53).

The writer of the book of Hebrews also presents life as a pilgrimage.

"All these people were still living by faith when they died. They did not receive the things promised; they only saw them and welcomed them from a distance. And they admitted that they were aliens and strangers on earth" (Hebrews 11:13).

The object of this plan was not only eternal salvation, but also the lifting of humankind from its selfish, sinful ways to a life of moral virtue and holiness. It was to restore an intimacy with God so that his image, his holiness might be seen in them. While kingdom citizens were on this pilgrimage, the Holy Spirit would be at work in them developing holiness, and through them, bringing beauty and love to others.

"But now he has reconciled you . . . to present you holy in his sight, without blemish . . . if you continue in your faith, established and firm, not moved from the hope held out in the gospel" (Col. 1:22-23).

In this great plan we see a God who is passionately involved in bringing his people to holiness of life. They are his family. They serve as his representatives in this world, spreading his love and glory, vastly enriching the present society. Then they will enter the eternal realms he has planned for them.

God's high hopes continue to prevail. He *will* have a holy people. They will come out of the crucible of earthly life. They will be those who chose to serve him and were led and nurtured by the Holy Spirit, until they "reflect the Lord's glory . . . being transformed into his likeness" (2 Cor. 3:18).

But how is this great transformation to take place? The remainder of this book will deal with that subject, so read on!

Discussion Starters:

1. Discuss this statement: The selfish tendency to lust, greed and pride exists in all people.
2. In what ways were the temptations of Eve and Jesus similar?

3. What are the three instincts (drives) dominant in the human nature?
4. What sins do these three instincts turn into when given priority in our lives?
5. What different methods did God use to progressively reveal his plan of redemption?
6. Did God's eternal plan include provision for man to live a holy life during his physical existence? How so?
7. In what sense is life a pilgrimage?
8. What impact would "pilgrims" have on the world as they passed through this life?

Chapter 4

Putting the Plan into Action

The unveiling of God's plan of redemption was gradual, like getting only one piece at a time of a giant jigsaw puzzle. It did not burst out suddenly after the Fall. It was only hinted at in the garden when God provided coverings of skin for his human creatures. Additional pieces came one at a time through the lives of the patriarchs, the judges, the kings, the poets, and the prophets.

The puzzle neared completion with the massive revelations by Jesus during his incarnation. The apostles' writings put in the final pieces. God's mysterious plan was then fully unveiled. To get the big picture, one needs to look at all the pieces, found in both the Old and New Testaments. Put together, it can be seen that God provided both a means for man to be forgiven and reconciled with himself, and a means by which man could be enabled by the Spirit of God to live a holy life.

This plan was audacious. It assumed that, even though humankind had become totally infected with evil, we could be wholly healed. It provided that, in spite of the depth of depravity that had come upon the race, and the sinister strength of the fallen human nature, we could be redeemed to live a holy life!

The Problem Defined

After the Fall, Adam and Eve and their descendants are described in the Bible as sinful. The Bible declares that every individual (none excepted) is evil in thought and deed. In fact, the race could only be identified by the word "evil".

"The Lord saw how great man's wickedness on earth had become, and that every inclination of the thoughts of his heart was only evil all the time. The Lord was grieved . . . and his heart was filled with pain" (Genesis 6:5-6).

This human condition, declared in the Bible, is confirmed in us today, individually and collectively. Selfishness permeates human behavior, resulting in every imaginable type of errant living. This selfishness is endemic, producing terrible violence, hatred, and suffering on the whole earth. Not only is it endemic, but it also seems invincible. Try as one might, the pulsating human drives for Pleasure, Possessions, and Position, continue to master us. Far from living the holy loving life God desires, all fall short and are guilty before a holy God. So God's redemption plan required a provision for overcoming the carnal human nature.

The plan also must address the need for forgiveness. Failure and guilt are a part of every human life. All have not only inherited a nature prone to selfishness and disobedience, but have also yielded to that nature and become sinful in word and deed. Pursuing our selfish desires for Pleasure, Possessions and Position has led to behavior unacceptable to God. As we age, the list of our offenses gets longer and longer. If not dealt with, they will lead not only to final judgment but also to a very unhappy life. Therefore, God's plan for redemption needed to include a provision for a just settlement for offenses and a forgiveness that brings deliverance from guilt.

While his plan deals mainly with the *process* of redemption, the *goal* of redemption must be kept in mind. God desires a people who live holy, righteous lives, where love for each other produces a society called the Kingdom of Heaven.

Righteous Living

The relationship between religion and morality has suffered through the centuries. While all religions espouse the concept of living a virtuous life, they tend to drift into rituals and worship patterns that have become ends in themselves, often giving little or no attention to the formation of character. One can go through all of the ceremonies of religious worship and come away feeling better, but not affected in regards to *lifestyle.* Religious activity can actually perpetuate immoral living by suggesting to the participants that God has been appeased by the activity, and they can now keep on living as they have been.

In Christianity, a person can be led to think that if he believes in Jesus, and trusts his death as atonement for his sin, he is immune from judgment. He is saved. Lifestyle does not matter! Add to this the teaching of some that everyone sins every day, and that sin is normal and only needs to be confessed. The result is an acceptance of behavior that is far from holy. These teachings have resulted in some Christian communities that differ little in lifestyle from the culture at large. Divorce, sexual perversion, and ethical failures are nearly as common with the churched as with the un-churched.

In his book, *After You Believe*, N. T. Wright says,

> "Basically the whole idea of virtue has been radically out of fashion in much of Western Christianity ever since the sixteenth century. Since we are justified through faith apart from works, why bother with all this morality?"

The author goes on to call for the development of virtuous character with a goal of becoming a just person

Sincere seekers for holiness are a counter-culture within the church at large. They cannot conceive of religion that does not affect lifestyle. To them, religion is all about serving God with a virtuous life. They look to God to help them overcome temptation, and to develop a Christian character, with Jesus as their model. This hunger for righteous living is an echo of the holiness in our first parents. All have this hunger to some degree. It is the thing that creates guilt when one does wrong. It is the thing that drives sincere seekers after God to press on in spite of their failures. This drive has produced saints down through the centuries. Many have found in God's redemption plan a provision of grace that has made them victorious, and holy!

Dual Deliverance

God's redemptive plan meets these two needs. It provides for both salvation and living a holy life. We find the salvation provision in the *death* of Christ. We find the holy living provision in the *life* of Christ.

Most sincere Christians understand God's plan concerning salvation. It has been clearly stated through the centuries since Jesus was crucified. His death was substitutionary, a final blood sacrifice for every individual and the sins of the whole world. This great act of love made possible forgiveness and reconciliation with God. Our part is to turn from sin in repentance, and to place his faith and trust in Christ. At that moment, God breathes again into the seeker, regenerating eternal life by imparting his Holy Spirit. The seeker is saved. Justice has been satisfied. A new life has begun.

God's redemptive plan also makes provision for living a holy life. This part of the plan is not as clearly understood. So much attention has been given to the death of Jesus Christ and the salvation it brings, that the significance of the life of Jesus Christ has been overshadowed and given comparative insignificance. The apostle Paul calls this to our attention.

"For if, when we were God's enemies, we were reconciled to him through the death of his Son, how much more, having been reconciled, shall we be saved through his life" (Romans 5:10)!

The salvation that comes through his *life* has to do with following the example he set while he was on earth. He was in a human body and yet lived a holy life. He is the only human being that did not sin. He demonstrated that it is possible to overcome the carnal human nature. By the way he lived he revealed a secret to holy living, a secret that when discovered and followed, can lead a sincere seeker to a similar victory over the flesh. This redemptive plan is God's way of putting it all back together, so we can live out the image of God.

Let's continue by considering how this new life begins.

Discussion Starters:

1. Is selfishness a problem for you? Is it a "pulsating human drive?"
2. What two provisions were included in God's redemption plan?
3. What is the ultimate goal of redemption?
4. What beliefs may cause one to minimize the importance of a moral life style?
5. In what way are we saved through the *life* of Jesus?

Chapter 5

Beginning the Journey

We are in a modern delivery room. A baby is about to be born. While those attending give their encouragement, the mother gives a final push. The baby is born. The groaning of the mother is replaced with the lusty cry of a newborn. Life has begun. All present are awed and thankful, and rejoicing erupts along with tears of relief. Another has begun its journey of life.

Each human being needs a second delivery-room experience. Spiritually dead in transgressions and sins, the soul needs spiritual regeneration, a resurrection from this death. This is why Jesus told Nicodemus, "Ye must be born again" (John 3:3). Spiritual rebirth is an event, a moment in time, when God breathes spiritual life back into the soul. It is a time of awe and rejoicing. It is the beginning of the journey to holiness.

Just as awe and wonder attend our first birth, mystery veils the second. We need to break through this veil and try to grasp how one is "born again." What happens in *that* delivery room?

One does not suddenly enter the spiritual delivery room. For most, new birth is preceded by months, and even years, of spiritual gestation. The Holy Spirit is at every juncture of one's life, patiently trying to show the foolishness of sin and the way of righteousness. He leads to the one who can deliver, the Lord Jesus Christ. His work within is like a seminal seed, full of potential, but dependent upon a cooperative response.

What response is necessary? What can a person, who is "dead in sins and transgressions" do to cooperate with the Holy Spirit? Actually, not much, unless God enables him. If such is the case, the response should be like that of Mary, who was challenged to cooperate with the Holy Spirit in connection with the conception of Jesus.

"'How will this be,' Mary asked the angel, 'since I am a virgin?' The angel answered, 'The Holy Spirit will come upon you, and the power of the Most High will overshadow you . . . For nothing is impossible with God.' 'I am the Lord's servant,' Mary answered. 'May it be to me as you have said'" (Luke 1:34-38).

Though our situation is different, it would not be wrong to imagine God replying to our question, "How can I be born again?" with the same answer He gave to Mary. "The Holy Spirit will come upon you, and the power of the Most High will overshadow you . . . for nothing is impossible with God."

Our response should be similar to Mary's: "May it be to me as you have said." We must believe God and be willing to submit to his plan. That God should come to her, speak to her, and work such a miracle in her, is the operation of God's grace. He is the active agent. But Mary had the option to cooperate or to refuse. Her faith and willingness is the type of attitude necessary if one is to experience the miracle of spiritual resurrection. Her response is a foreshadowing of the type of submission that is required if one is to live the holy life.

Specifically, just what does it mean to submit to God in our spiritual regeneration? What is our role in this miraculous moment? The Bible presents two clear answers, *repentance* and *faith.*

Repentance

Repentance has to do with the battle Adam and Eve faced in the garden, that is, "submission/obedience versus rebellion/disobedience" (Chapter 3). Their relationship with God was severed because they chose the rebellion/disobedience route. In order for spiritual life to be restored, that choice must be reversed. A reversal of our choice to the way of submission/obedience is called repentance.

God's appeal through the centuries has been for man to repent.

"And if they have a change of heart in the land where they are held captive, and repent and plead with you . . . and say, 'We have sinned, we have done wrong, we have acted wickedly,' and if they turn back to you with all their heart and soul . . . then from heaven, your dwelling place, hear their prayer . . . and forgive your people" (1 Kings 8:47-50).

"In those days John the Baptist came, preaching . . . 'Repent, for the kingdom of heaven is near'" (Matt. 3:1).

Repentance is a reversal of direction. Too often it is seen as only a sorrow for sin, a sense of remorse for having failed, a plea for forgiveness. It is all of this, but even more fundamentally, it is a decision which involves turning from willful rebellion against God. It is turning to God with the idea of obeying him, following him and going his way from that moment on.

Many turn a deaf ear to this call to repentance. They have become so hardened in their hearts that attempts by the Holy Spirit to get through are either ignored or rejected. Nevertheless, the Holy Spirit continues with great kindness and patience to bring a person to his senses.

"Or do you show contempt for the riches of his kindness, tolerance and patience, not realizing that God's kindness leads you toward repentance" (Romans 2:4).

Those who do hear the call to repent, who recognize the truth of the Holy Spirit's message, and who begin to consider repenting, are well on their way to new birth. But there is more that is required in this matter of spiritual regeneration than repentance.

Faith

Faith is the second response God is seeking. It is an essential element to the new birth. Circumstances of life can work to destroy faith in God. God the Holy Spirit, on the other hand, works to restore faith in God. While we are still in sin, his gracious influence seeks to remind us that there is a God who cares. He plants the seeds of faith in us.

Faith is a gift God brings to fruition in us when he sees we have truly repented. Often our doubts are rationalizations to excuse a sinful lifestyle. It is normal for the person who is not living right, and who has a measure of guilt because of it, to avoid facing the real problem by denying the faith. They will say, "I can't believe," when the truth is that they do not want to believe because if they did, they would then have to change. When one is ready to abandon his selfish lifestyle, disbelief often dissolves, liberating a faith that has been there all the time. Whatever the process, the revival of faith is crucial.

The necessity of faith is demonstrated by the heavy emphasis Jesus placed upon it.

"If that is how God clothes the grass of the field, which is here today and tomorrow is thrown into the fire, will he not much more clothe you, O you of little faith" (Matt. 6:30)?

"For John came to show you the way of righteousness, and you did not believe him, but the tax collectors and the prostitutes did. And even after you saw this, you did not repent and believe him" (Matt. 21:32).

Faith is one of the central themes in the Bible.

"Abraham believed the Lord, and he credited it to him as righteousness" (Gen. 15:6).

". . . but the righteous will live by his faith" (Hab. 2:4).

"And without faith it is impossible to please God, because anyone who comes to him must believe that he exists and that he rewards those who earnestly seek him" (Heb. 11:6).

The Apostle John is even more specific. He says our faith must be in the Lord Jesus Christ.

"Whoever believes in the Son has eternal life, but whoever rejects the Son will not see life, for God's wrath remains on him" (John 3:36).

"Yet to all who received him (Jesus), to those who believed in his name, he gave the right to become children of God" (John 1:12).

Putting one's faith in God is just as much an attitude change as repentance. It means that rather than depending upon our own efforts to survive (and to please God), we decide instead to depend on God's mercy, and the provision he has made for our forgiveness and regeneration. This provision is his son Jesus, who by his death made atonement for our sin. Faith says, "I believe Jesus died in my place, taking the punishment for my sins, so now I can be forgiven."

"In him we have redemption through his blood, the forgiveness of sins, in accordance with the riches of God's grace . . ." (Eph. 1:7).

Jesus not only died to atone for our sins, but he rose again and became the source of the new life to our dead souls.

"But because of his great love for us, God, who is rich in mercy, made us alive with Christ even when we were dead in transgressions—it is by grace you have been saved. And God raised us up with Christ" (Eph. 2:4-6).

With this understanding of both faith and repentance, an understanding that usually comes gradually as the Holy Spirit works in us, we are ready to be born again. It can happen anywhere. The moment of repentance comes. We make our prayer, asking for forgiveness and pledge to try and change our way of life. We invite Christ to come in, and place our faith in God's grace and provision. Then the miracle happens. God forgives us. Our spiritual life is revived. Our relationship with God is restored. We have been born again. Angels rejoice. A soul has begun the journey that is to lead to a holy life.

A Christmas poem I once wrote captures the wonder and essence of one's new birth.

My Own Nativity

The advent of the ages was not in eons past,
Not in a stable lowly, when Jesus came at last,
But then this simple seeker asked Him to enter in—
And wonder of all wonders, the babe was born within.

That germ of life so fertile, that potent little spark,
That essence of divinity was born within my heart.
Though wrapped in flesh so lowly and scarcely recognized,
In time He owned me fully, my life revitalized.

As shepherds heard the angels when Jesus first arrived,
I also heard them singing the day I came alive.
They sang of peace for all men, of joy and hope, good will;
The shepherds only heard it; I received it to the full.

The advent of the ages was not in eons past,
And Christmas celebrations for me are ever cast
In this another advent, the one that came to me
When Jesus came from heaven; my own nativity.

This is just the beginning. Although this new life is fragile and needs much care, it is endowed with the potential to become the holy person God is seeking.

Discussion Starters:

1. Can you identify the moment you were saved? Where? When?
2. What is the "spiritual gestation" period? How long does it last?
3. What is God's role in the new birth? Man's role?
4. Describe the meaning of "repentance."
5. Describe the meaning of "faith."
6. Do all people who have been born again have a "miracle" moment when they experience new birth?

Chapter 6

Beyond Conversion

Even though a new baby brings much joy at birth, it can do little more. It is so small, so helpless, so dependent. But what potential it has! In that living baby are the genes of generations, the embryonic endowments of a gracious God, the capacity to learn, to grow, to become. Someone has said, "You can count the seeds in an apple, but you can't count the apples in a seed." So it is with each baby. No one can begin to imagine all that will transpire from that one life. Though small and unproved now, it contains the wherewithal to become great.

The same may be said of the person who has just been "born again." In many ways, the second delivery room experience is similar to the first. The result is new life fraught with immense potential, but for the time being, very dependent, and even fragile. That new life in the soul, the renewal of God's presence within, brings with it the genes of God's Holiness, the embryonic endowment of spiritual gifts, and the capacity to grow, to learn, to become. Although very much a "babe in Christ" now, it has the wherewithal to mature spiritually, to become holy.

Holy in Status

The new convert has started down the road to holiness. God sees the new convert as holy, as a saint, as sanctified (set apart) since he now belongs to Him. We are holy by status with God, if not holy in lifestyle. In his book, *Never The Same Again*, General Shaw Clifton, Retd., describes this well.

"You became holy by status in the same sense that Paul says the far-from-perfect recipients of his letters were holy. For most Christians the gap between holy status and holy living is at first a very wide one. Growing in grace and in spiritual maturity is about closing that gap, steadily but surely."

Maturing is a slow process. We recognize this to be so for the newborn baby. The early euphoria of the baby's arrival soon gives way to the unrelenting demands that go with helping the baby to grow. Long nights for the parents stretch out into long years of patiently caring, curbing, and counseling. They nurture and guide the growing child through many stages of development until the child becomes a mature adult, independent, and equipped to enter into his or her life's work.

Becoming spiritually mature is a quite similar process. The early euphoria and joy that comes with the new birth usually fades. It is common for difficulties to arise as the newborn tries to change his behavioral patterns. Hopefully he is loved and supported during this time by patient Christian friends. He also has the ever present help of the Holy Spirit within who guides, protects, and strengthens. The new child of God will pass through many stages in his development, all moving him onward toward becoming mature, holy like his Father.

Learning to Eat, Walk, and Talk

One of the very first processes in early development is learning how to eat, learning how to nurture the new life within. Nourishment will at first be the care and encouragement from Christian friends. Their love, guidance, and prayer will often make the difference between living and dying in those early days. But soon the newborn learns to feed itself. He chooses music that is encouraging and uplifting. He learns to listen, and to absorb helpful things from conversations with other Christians, from Christian radio and TV, and from the sermons at church. But the most significant evidence of having learned to feed himself is when he begins to regularly read the Bible in a meditative mood, allowing God to move in his heart as he reads. Such a diet of good friends, good reading, good listening and Bible devotions will contribute to the development of this babe in Christ.

Another part of this early development is learning to walk. The baby crawls a while but soon is able to stand erect and toddle around. It takes a while, but before long, the little child has become a "holy terror" racing around with complete abandon. It also takes a while for the newborn child of God to learn how to walk. Learning to walk marks the passage from passive observance to active participation.

Just how is this new life to be lived out? What will be its goals, its purposes? Learning to walk means a lot of trial and error. False starts and frequent tumbles are normal. Gradually though, the young Christian learns what it means to "walk the talk." Active participation will eventually include helping others, being kind and compassionate, sharing, being honest, becoming a helpful part of a church fellowship, and going on to serve God in the particular way he directs. As this walk becomes stronger, the child of God has begun to make progress toward the holiness God desires.

Learning to talk (communicate) is also a part of normal development. For the young Christian this means developing the ability to communicate with both God and man. Prayer and sharing one's testimony at first will be difficult and simple. But with repeated attempts speaking improves. Early prayers will be quite simple expressions of love, praise, and pleas for help. These simple words are as delightful to God as the early words of a baby are to its parents. God knows that eventually he will learn to talk better.

The gist of what is being said here is that after being made spiritually alive in Christ, there follows a time of gradual spiritual development. It is true that the newborn child of God is adopted into God's family, is fully forgiven and cleansed of all guilt for his sin (justified), is set apart for God's purposes (sanctified), is a full joint-heir with Christ of the eternal kingdom, is indwelt by the Holy Spirit, but he has still just barely begun the new life. There is so much to learn, so much growth to take place, and many hurdles to overcome as he moves on toward holiness.

A Spiritual Battle

One tremendous hurdle that the newborn Christian has, which has no equivalent in the infant, is a deeply fixed pattern of living which needs to be changed. Regardless of how old one is at the time of his conversion, the selfish habits of life will be deeply entrenched. These habits, both mental and physical, will cling tenaciously and resist every effort to change. The new spiritually alive person has basically the same personality after rebirth as before with the exception that now he has set his heart on going with God. His focus has changed and guilt has gone, but those old problems that bring much grief and shame are still there.

It soon becomes obvious that the Christian life is not going to be easy. Old habits die hard. Tears and despair may accompany frequent failure. But, like a baby learning to walk, the new Christian gets up again after each tumble and keeps trying. Falls, and defeats by old habits, are not an indication that he has left God or that God has left him, but rather that he is still trying. The only real failure would be if the person gave up on his desire to go with God and turned deliberately back to his old ways of rebellion and sin. God, however, cheers him on, giving his encouragement after each fall, and his affirmation after every sign of progress. Gradually victories become more frequent than failures. The child has begun to grow, gaining new strength every day. But the battle is not yet over.

The Carnal Nature Prevails

While repentance at the time of one's spiritual regeneration means a change of one's attitude toward sin, the deeper problem of the residual effect of the carnal nature has not been addressed. In fact, it may not even be recognized to exist until one begins to struggle to change. With the struggle comes an awareness that the source of sin and failure lies deep within. Strong inclinations after Pleasure, Possessions, and Position dominate the life. Lust, greed and pride bubble up naturally. They seem to be a "law of life" that cannot be broken. Basic self-interest and self-centeredness result in selfish actions. It seems like one is chained to a body of death, destined to an existence of frustration, wanting to be good, but doomed to falling short. Thoughts of becoming holy are gradually set aside. A time of feeling miserable is not unusual. The enemy has been identified, and seems to be invincible.

At this point, most honest seekers enter into a sort of accommodation stage, an adjustment to the conflict between high desires and human weakness. Even though the Bible calls them on to holy living, the powerful drag of the fallen human nature seems to say this is impossible. So one settles in to living a life to the best he can, but compromised often by failure. It is not hard to become cynical, and reject the idea of holiness.

Every new day is marred on waking by selfish urges, the driving desire for personal Pleasure, ease, comfort, sensual gratification; the driving desire for Possessions, the longing to acquire things, to have a better home, car, boat, clothes, money; the driving desire for Position, battles with jealousy, ambition, recognition, one's own turf. These God-given instincts (see Chapter 2), so necessary for the survival of the race, have turned rogue and fight tooth and nail to continue their dominance. The carnal drives of lust, greed and pride have become second nature. Their dominion is so strong, that most seekers never get past this hurdle. They settle for a sort of combination of right living and frequent failure, thinking this is probably the best it can ever be.

Questionable Cures

Religionists of every ilk have faced the problem of the carnal nature and developed a variety of theories promising deliverance. They range from severe discipline and asceticism to a miraculous removal. Some focus on fervent emotional experiences and some on a lifelong process of striving. For some the problem is compounded by the disillusionment that comes from trying promised cures. Many seekers try the "cures" but find, after some effort, that they just don't work. Nothing has changed. The old problem is still there. It often happens that the honest seeker, not only becomes disillusioned, but also calloused, especially if he or she had repeatedly tried these ineffective "cures."

We have arrived at the very crux of the business of becoming holy. If we are going to press on to that holiness of heart God intends for mankind, that holiness which God longs to see in us, then we are going to have to find his plan for living a holy life while in a human body. There is such a plan, and it is revealed in the life of Jesus, who did live a holy life in a human body. In the next two chapters we shall try to discover how his mindset made this possible.

Discussion Starters:

---

1. Share about the greatest joy you ever had over a baby being born.
2. In what ways are the birth of a baby and being born again similar?
3. What is the status with God of a newly born again Christian?
4. What is there in the human nature that powerfully resists efforts to change?
5. Do you agree that many Christians settle for something less than living a holy life? Why is this so?
6. Name some religious "cures" that have not produced the desired results.

Chapter 7

The Importance of Mindset

We are told in the Bible of two rich men who had different value systems. One was holy, a joy to God. The other was worldly, eventually lost. The first was Job, and the other was the rich man in one of Jesus' stories.

The set of one's mind, the value system he has adopted and lives by, is a key factor in the quest for holiness. What one really wants, what he values highest, determines his mindset. It is the things upon which we have set our minds. These desires, to which we give priority, form what we call our *mindset.*

The Apostle Paul clearly indicates that the solution to the wretched condition of the saved person struggling with a carnal body is a changed set of the mind. This "wretchedness" is described by Paul as seeking holiness through self-discipline.

"So I find this law at work: When I want to do good, evil is right there with me. For in my inner being I delight in God's law, but I see another law at work in the members of my body, waging war against the law of my mind and making me a prisoner of the law of sin at work within my members. What a wretched man I am" (Romans 7:21-24)!

Paul indicates that the key to victory over the carnal nature is not in tight self-discipline but in the proper set of the mind. Those who are in Christ and led by his Spirit gain victory through the proper set of the mind.

"Therefore, there is now no condemnation for those who . . . do not live according to the sinful nature but according to the Spirit. Those who live according to the sinful nature have their *minds set* on what that nature desire; but those who live in accordance with the Spirit have their *minds set* on what the Spirit desires" (Romans 8:1, 5).

These verses suggest a new word for our consideration. It is *mindset.* It suggests that the set of our mind, the values we hold dearest, the ruling desires in our heart, are the key to gaining victory over the carnal nature. When we set our mind on what the Spirit desires we have life and peace. Ella Wheeler Wilcox affirmed this when she wrote,

> "One ship sails east, the other sails west
> By the selfsame wind that blows.
> But it is the set of the sails
> And not of the gales
> That determines the way it goes."

As long as we concentrate on performance, trying to live a holy life, we will be frustrated. But when we focus on keeping spiritual values supreme in the heart, we will find peace and steady improvement. It is the set of the soul—the values that one establishes as paramount—that affects the way one goes. Mindset determines destiny. We cannot hope to become holy in lifestyle until we give proper attention to the set of our minds. This is seen in the lives of the two rich men referred to earlier.

Job, a heroic saint of an early time, was one of these men. He was very rich, called the greatest man in the East. In fact, God bragged on him.

"Have you considered my servant Job? There is no one on earth like him; he is blameless and upright, a man who fears God and shuns evil" (Job 1:8).

Another translation of the Bible calls him "perfect." It is obvious that God was very pleased with Job. The terms "blameless," "upright," and "perfect," are all Bible synonyms for "holy." Job was a man God considered holy.

What was it about Job that God should consider him holy? No reference is made here to his avoidance of idol worship, to being a man of prayer, to keeping himself morally pure, to reading and keeping the law, to making many sacrifices. Job may have done all of these, but that was not what God saw as most important. What was it? It was his mindset, the ruling values in his life. God referred to these ruling principles. Job feared God (to fear is to serve, obey, honor and glorify) and shunned evil (turned his back to those things displeasing to God). It was because of this mindset, that God considered Job perfect.

A study of Job's life reveals that he was not perfect in his performance. He questioned God and even wished himself dead, but never relinquished his spiritual values. He kept his mind set on the things of God, even through severe human suffering.

It is almost as if God is saying to us here, "I accept as inevitable the fact that your performance is not going to be perfect. But if I can see that in your heart of hearts your supreme desire is after me, then as far as I am concerned, you are perfect." *God looks not on performance as much as he looks on motives,* and when he sees that the intent is to serve and honor him, he considers us holy! At least he did Job.

The other man described in a parable told by Jesus, is called The Rich Fool. He had a bumper crop one year and wondered where to store it.

"Then he said, 'This is what I'll do. I will tear down my barns and build bigger ones, and there I will store all my grain and my goods. And I'll say to myself, 'You have plenty of good things laid up for many years. Take life easy; eat drink and be merry'" (Luke 12:18-19).

There is no doubt about his mindset. Material goods, ease, and pleasure were the things that counted most with him. No praise or affirmation came from God for him. In fact, he is called a fool.

"But God said to him, 'You fool! This very night your life will be demanded from you. Then who will get what you have prepared for yourself'" (Luke 12:20)?

Compare these two men, one condemned, one approved. Materially they both had prospered. But when the testing time came, they were evaluated on the basis of their mindset.

One of the key words God used to describe Job was "blameless" (Job 1:8). The concept of blamelessness plays a major role in our consideration of holiness. This concept infers that God will not consider us guilty or blameworthy if our mindset is right (if we do not sin willfully) even when our performance is not perfect. If what we do proceeds from a heart that is right, even though it may have the outward appearance of selfishness (sin), God seeing the intent, assigns no blame.

"Keep your servant also from willful sins; may they not rule over me. Then will I be blameless, innocent of great transgression" (Psalm 19:13).

Notice that David feels he is blameless if he has committed no willful sins. From his youth David had his heart set on God. The Psalms he has written give witness to his close relationship with God and his longing to keep the Lord first in his life. From his writing it is obvious that he was at peace with God. He did not feel perfect, but he did feel blameless. That is, until he sinned willfully. His carnal human nature got the best of him and he chose to sin to satisfy himself. Then the sense of "blamelessness" was gone, and he grieved and repented and tearfully sought to be cleansed and purified.

Living blameless before God is also a New Testament theme.

"May God himself . . . sanctify you through and through. May your whole spirit, soul and body be kept blameless at the coming of our Lord Jesus Christ" (1 Thess. 5:23).

In the last reference, considered to be a foundational verse in regard to sanctification and holiness, it must be noted that there is not a hint that performance will be perfect, but only that after sanctification there will be the possibility of "blamelessness" in the sight of God.

The Biblical concept of blamelessness is always linked with intent. It must not be considered license to do what we please, masking evil desires behind some sort of imputed righteousness. Instead, it is God's way of responding to those errors of judgment and human frailties that inadvertently happen to those whose hearts are perfect toward him. To those who experience such failures, they are a cause of grief and a determination to do better. God, seeing this attitude of the heart, considers that one blameless, and continues his abiding presence and peace in that life.

Since the proper mindset is so essential to holiness, we must ask, "How do we go about getting this proper mindset?" We will answer this question in Chapter 9, but first we will take a look at the mindset of Jesus during his time in a human body. His mindset establishes the pattern for all who would live a holy life in this world.

Discussion Starters:

1. Have you ever gotten lost? How did you find your way again?
2. How does Paul say we can get victory over our carnal nature? Does this make sense to you?

3. Describe what is meant by "mindset."
4. Do you agree with the statement: "Mindset determines destiny?"
5. Why did Job please God? In what sense was he perfect?
6. When does God consider us *blameless*?

Chapter 8

The Mindset of Jesus

A repeated and urgent theme in much of Christian literature and hymnody calls for the believer to "be like Jesus." Holiness is often described as being like Jesus. In his books, Commissioner Samuel Logan Brengle says that the essence of holiness is, in one word, *Christlikeness.* We are urged in the Scriptures to be imitators of Jesus, to do as we think Jesus would do. While we may long to be like Jesus, and try hard to follow his example, we don't do very well at it! It is as hard for us to be like Jesus as it would be for a novice golfer to be like a PGA champion.

Many who want to be like Jesus are confused. What was Jesus really like? They have little concept of how Jesus lived and what it means to be like him. They encounter situations where it is difficult to know how Jesus would react. At best, interpretations of how Jesus would respond are highly subjective. The questions often revolve around what Jesus would *do* (performance), and suggest answers beyond our ability.

The answer to this confusion is found in the fact that we are called, not to duplicate Jesus' actions, but his mindset. The locus of holiness is in the set of the mind. If we can only get his values paramount in our desires and thinking, our actions will take care of themselves. The Apostle Paul repeatedly emphasized the set of the mind.

"Your attitude should be the same as that of Christ Jesus" (Phil. 2:6).

The word "attitude" is translated in KJV to read, "Let this *mind* be in you." The actual Greek word in this text is a word that means, "exercise the mind." The above text could be translated, "Exercise your mind so that it is the same as that of Christ Jesus." The same word is used in Paul's letter to the Colossians.

"Set your mind (affections) on things above and not on earthly things" (Col. 3:2).

Jesus' mind was set on heavenly values which enabled him to humble himself, even to death on the cross. We make a mistake if we try to mimic the actions of Jesus, but ignore his mindset. So, let us try to flesh out his mindset. What was the setting of his mind that enabled him to live a holy life?

Like the rest of us, Jesus inherited a human nature. Born of a human mother, he started out with the basic human desires common to us all. If we believe that he was "truly and properly man" (as does most of the Christian church) then he, too, knew the tremendous pull of the God-given natural human desires for Pleasure, Possessions, and Position.

This was clearly confirmed by the way Satan tempted him in the wilderness experience at the beginning of his ministry (Luke 4:1-13). By directing temptations to these three areas, Satan unwittingly confirmed the humanity of Jesus. He must have felt Jesus would be vulnerable. But Jesus had another set of values, a different *mindset.* It is obvious that Jesus had come to terms with the normal human drives and was determined that they would not dominate his life.

How did Jesus come to such determination? If he were to identify fully with our dilemma, he must have had a struggle like ours, deciding what he wanted most in life. It was not any easier for him than for us. The lure of things in this world is so strong. We can only guess at the battles Jesus had. We can imagine the stress and tests of his early childhood, normal sibling competition, and resistance to parental authority. But very early in life he had sorted things out. He would not live for the things of this world, but instead for the things of God. How or when this happened we do not know, yet it is obvious that he had a different mindset and a changed value system when we first meet him in the Gospel records.

This higher set of values which he adopted, this different mindset, is first noticed on his trip to the temple with his parents at age 12. He felt he "must be about his Father's business." Very early in his life, it was obvious that he would live by a different set of values.

The seeming ease with which Jesus overcame Satan's temptations reveals that he was already clear in his focus. You might say his "eye was single," that is, there was no ambivalence in his purposes. He had a mindset which would keep him on course. This clear focus on a different set of values coupled with reliance on God for help, constituted the basis from which Jesus was able to live a holy life in a human body.

What was his mindset? What values did he choose to place first in his life? If we can identify these we will have a great advantage in our own quest for holiness. In fact we are urged to have this *same* mindset. Although he never came right out and outlined the principles which guided his life, we can deduce them from his actions and his teachings. Here are three values that dominated his life.

Glorify His Father

Would Jesus live to please himself, or to please his heavenly Father? Would he live to seek his own honor, dominated by personal ambition, or would he live to bring honor and glory to his

Father? Certainly he did not want to shame his heavenly Father. He was concerned that his life be a credit to him, one that would glorify him.

Children can disgrace their parents by the way they live their lives. Many have cared little about how their actions reflected on their parents. Their quest for Pleasure has led them down the paths of lust and indulgence, with the result that mom and dad are not only heart broken but also embarrassed. Shamed!

While Jesus would be mindful of his earthly parents, it was his heavenly Father he was most concerned about. He called him Father and had a supreme desire to live his life in such a way that he would be a credit to him. He wanted his life to glorify God, to be a reflection of his holiness in all that he did and said.

"I do nothing on my own but speak just what the Father taught me . . . for I always do what pleases him" (John 8:28-29).

This desire is evident when Jesus prayed at the last supper, facing his approaching crucifixion.

"After Jesus said this, he looked toward heaven and prayed, 'Father, the time has come. Glorify your son, that your son may glorify you . . . I have brought you glory on earth by completing the work you gave me to do'" (John 17:1,4).

Years later, theologians wrote in the Westminster Shorter Catechism that the "Man's chief end is to glorify God and to enjoy Him forever." Jesus knew and lived this long before. This desire to glorify God is the foundation of all spiritual principles. It is diametrically opposed to the carnal desire to please self, to gratify the carnal desires. Once firmly espoused, it provides a dynamic criterion for determining the rightness or wrongness of any contemplated action. "Would this bring glory to God, please him, or is this something for my pleasure, with a price tag of shame attached?" Is it any wonder Satan failed when he asked Jesus to use his supernatural powers to make bread to satisfy his own hunger? The thought rang alarm bells in Jesus' value system. He had no trouble. The decision had been made long ago. One key element to his mindset was: "Live to God's glory."

Fulfill His Destiny

Most of us will identify with a sense of destiny; we feel we are put on this earth for a purpose. Something within motivates us to live right so we might achieve this purpose. We may not know what this purpose is, and for many it may be veiled in mystery much of their lives, but nevertheless, it is there. Jesus, as a growing child, must have been moved with the same feelings. Perhaps his mother or other relatives had shared with him the miraculous events that surrounded his birth. He would have learned early about the heroes of the Old Testament, men and women sent by God with a definite work to do. By the time he was twelve, he sensed God had some "business" for him to take care of. It is obvious that at some point Jesus had determined to put God's business first in his life. This was another key element in his mindset: "Do God's Will."

Was it hard for Jesus to adopt this crucial value? Again we can only speculate. If he was fully human, and if Satan thought he could lure him with the ideas of fame and fortune, then he must have had the same yearnings we have, to plot our own course, to do our own thing, to follow our own ambitions and dreams. Jesus may have wrestled with these same thoughts. We have no record of when this value became important to him, but it is obvious from his later actions and statements that he had fought and won this battle. He was fully committed to doing the will of God.

He clearly told his disciples that he was on a mission.

"'My food,' said Jesus, 'is to do the will of Him who sent me and to finish his work'" (John 4:34).

He sensed his destiny; he had a job to do.

"'You are king then!' said Pilate. Jesus answered, 'you are right . . . in fact, for this reason I was born, and for this I came into the world, to testify to the truth'" (John 18:37).

"For even the Son of Man did not come to be served, but to serve, and to give his life as a ransom for many'" (Mark 10:45).

This awareness of a destiny to fulfill, a work to do, and the commitment to do it, permeated his life right up to the end, requiring the ultimate surrender of his life.

"He withdrew about a stone's throw beyond them, knelt down and prayed, 'Father, if you are willing, take this cup from me; yet not my will, but yours be done' . . . and his sweat was like drops of blood falling to the ground" (Luke 22:42-44).

What mattered most to Jesus was doing the will of God regardless of the cost. Armed with this determination he was equipped to overcome Satan's temptations. Jesus felt his role was to be that of servant, humbly doing the will of his master. He took on the form of a servant, humbled himself and became obedient to death. What a far cry from the power plays that dominate the affairs of men. This attitude, to do God's will, was another key to his holy life as a human.

Be a Blessing

Perhaps the most obvious aspect of Jesus' mindset, was his compassionate caring for all people. Jesus was the epitome of patience and concern. He welcomed and touched those with repulsive diseases. He stood beside the condemned and offered forgiveness. He fed the hungry multitudes. He visited in the homes of the needy. He took time for people who came to him, regardless of his own weariness. He was determined to be a blessing, to reach out in love. He sensed his calling was to radiate the love of God to all he met.

It is said of Jesus that when he left heaven to come to earth, he emptied himself of everything but love. That is, he divested

Himself of all his divine majesty and power, just keeping a heart to love. This seems credible in view of the way he lived his life. But was love automatic in the child Jesus? Children are so naturally selfish and often cruel. What mother has not wondered if her fighting children would ever learn to be loving and kind? Teaching to share, to be considerate, to be helpful, are all major lessons to be learned. If Jesus was fully human, then he must have been an active participant in the give and take of the Mary/Joseph household, with its many children.

If he was all boy, how can we account for his maturing into a loving adult life? We can only assume that at some point in his development, Jesus made a decision that affected the direction of his life. The love that resided in him as the divine Son of God would become a ruling principle in his life. It may not have been obvious overnight to his family, but by the time Jesus began his ministry, it was. He cared deeply about people and wanted to use his life and resources to bless them. This helps us to see that another key element in his mindset was, "Be a Blessing."

It is in the loving life of Jesus that we find our greatest inspiration for the life of holiness. He had a mission to accomplish, and there is no doubt that he had "set (his) face like flint" to accomplish it. (See Isa. 50:7). But, that did not prevent him from being kind, loving, helpful, and thoughtful of others while he was on the way!

In fact, the study of the early years of his ministry seems to indicate that his *primary* goal in life was to be a blessing, to heal, encourage, and teach, so others could find fullness of life. It was only later that his life-mission began to be seen, that of dying as the atonement for our sins. His life was one of giving himself constantly to be a blessing. Love flowed as from a fountain out of his life.

"The Spirit of the Lord is on me . . . to preach good news to the poor . . . the prisoners . . . the blind . . . the oppressed" (Luke 4:18).

What mattered were his friends and neighbors, those who needed him. Eventually he endured being spit upon, tortured, and crucified for these very people.

"Greater love has no man than this, that he lay down his life for his friends" (John 15:13).

The Holiness Mindset

Jesus marched to the beat of a different drum. In his heart was the steady cadence of the three cardinal values he had adopted.

1. Live to the Father's Glory
2. Do the Father's Will
3. Be a Blessing in the Father's Name

These values formulated the mindset of Jesus. They were the ruling principles of his life. All his decisions and actions were guided and controlled by these values. While normal human creatures march to the drum-beat of self gratification for Pleasure, Possessions, and Position, things of this world, Jesus placed his supreme values on pleasing God and focusing on the things of the spiritual world.

The result was a holy life. He lived with steady victory over temptation, not because of much self flagellation, or long ascetic retreats, or prolonged prayer and meditation, or severe self discipline, but because of his clear focus. These things all have their place, but Jesus lived a holy life in the midst of the most demanding circumstances because he had his mind set on the things of God. Certainly, the correct mindset is the way to a holy life.

Can such a mindset become ours? Now let us see how it can be so.

Discussion Starters:

1. Have you ever tried the WWJD plan? Did it work?
2. Do scriptures encourage us to imitate Jesus' actions, or his mindset?
3. What indication is there in Luke 4 that Jesus had a human nature like ours?
4. How did Jesus come to have a changed mindset? When?
5. What were the three ruling principles that guided Jesus' actions? Discuss the significance of each one.
6. Discuss: "The correct mindset is the way to a holy life."

Chapter 9

Changing Our Mindset

The secret of Jesus' ability to resist temptation and live a holy life was his mindset. His value system kept him on course, giving the motivation to love and serve, and warning him when temptations came. If his ability to live a holy life was so linked to his mindset, it follows that the person who wants to live a holy life would be well advised to adopt the value system of Jesus as his own.

Changing one's values is not easy. We are tightly attached to the values of the carnal nature. They are so much a part of us, and so intertwined with everything we have ever thought and done, that to reject them completely is not unlike dying. Many have called this transaction the "death of self." Most of those who have found the life of holiness tell of a personal struggle, a time of wrestling within, as one by one the values of Pleasure, Possessions, and Position have been reluctantly dethroned.

"Before we can pray and really mean it, 'Thy Kingdom come, Thy will be done', we must be willing to pray, 'My Kingdom go.'" (Allen Redpath)

Such a transaction tends to be a crisis experience, a critical moment that marks the beginning of an unconditionally surrendered life. Some call it a second work of grace, comparing it to the divine touch of regeneration that comes when one repents and puts his faith in Christ for salvation. It is the moment of supreme consecration, when one totally sets himself apart (sanctifies himself) for God's purposes.

This high moment of value-change, of putting on a new mindset is not a simple thing. It is so comprehensive that it cannot be undertaken lightly. It is important that we thoroughly understand all of its implications before we enter in.

The Bible gives several metaphors and examples. All of them underscore the comprehensive scope of this change, and help us to see that holiness is a matter of giving all. Four such instances are:

1. Jesus leaving heaven
2. The living sacrifice model
3. Jesus going to Calvary
4. The death/resurrection simile

Jesus Leaving Heaven

The pre-incarnation glory of Jesus in the heavenly realms can only be surmised. As one of the Godhead, he shared in all the joys and glories of the divine. This high and holy place he willingly surrendered to become our Savior. We are encouraged by the Apostle Paul to have the same attitude Jesus had in being willing to leave all.

"Your attitude should be the same as that of Christ Jesus; who, being in very nature God, did not consider equality with God something to be grasped, but made himself nothing, taking the very nature of a servant, being made in human likeness" (Phil 2:5-7).

We can only imagine what it cost Jesus to leave heaven to become a man. What were his circumstances? What were the depths of his relationships? What was his involvement in the governing of the universe? Whatever the sum total of these things, he did not feel these were things to be tightly grasped. Instead, his attitude was a willingness to let them all go. He was willing to make himself nothing, to become a servant.

This is the attitude that is to be in us. Note that the focus here is on his mindset (attitude). Paul commends his value system and says we should emulate it. We are not to grasp tightly what is ours, but hold all things loosely, ready to suffer the loss of all to do the will and work of God. It implies a mindset that values, as most important, pleasing God and not ourselves.

The Sacrifice Model

The worship of the Israelites centered on the altar of sacrifice. The sight of the knife plunged into an animal, its life blood flowing out, and the animal dying, was a scene they had witnessed many times. It was a repeated scene in which commitment was absolute and final. The sacrificial animal was sanctified fully to be the required offering.

The Apostle Paul saw in this ritual a model for the commitment that would precede being "transformed by the renewing of the mind."

"Therefore, I urge you, brothers, in view of God's mercy, to offer your bodies as living sacrifices, holy and pleasing to God—this is your spiritual act of worship. Do not conform any longer to the pattern of this world" (Romans 12:1-2).

While Paul knew that there was no need for further sacrifice for sin, he saw in the sacrificial system a pattern for Christian commitment. He called upon followers of Jesus to make a once and forever spiritual commitment of their lives, to be living sacrifices. To those originally hearing him, Paul is suggesting that the knife was to be plunged into the old way of life (the pursuit of carnal goals) until one was dead to them.

This presents a dramatic picture of one, who in a spiritual sense, has offered all to God in self sacrifice, but is now alive to live a life of service. He is speaking of a new mindset here, indicating that when this happens one will be holy and pleasing to God. Paul had experienced this personally.

"I have been crucified with Christ and I no longer live, but Christ lives in me. The life I live in the body, I live by faith in the Son of God, who loved me and gave himself for me" (Gal. 2:20).

Paul experienced this initial sacrifice as a dramatic moment in his life, but also taught that we never really get off the altar of sacrifice. He indicated that he "died daily."

"As for us, why do we endanger ourselves every hour: I die every day—I mean that brothers—just as surely as I glory over you in Christ Jesus our Lord" (1 Cor. 15:30-31).

He also said that he struggled to "keep the body under" at all times (1 Cor. 9:27). He mentioned the need for constant renewal of this commitment. He tells how this sacrificial attitude is maintained.

"Do not conform any longer to the pattern of this world, but be transformed by the renewing of your mind" (Romans 12:2).

Here is another reference to the importance of the mindset. Keeping our mindset renewed is a means to being transformed. It is as if he were saying that the body keeps trying to crawl off the altar, and that we must work to keep it there, to be a living sacrifice, to daily reject giving supremacy to human drives, and daily affirm our new mindset.

Jesus Going to Calvary

If the previous examples throw only a dim light on the full commitment necessary to holiness, a bright light is found in the example of Jesus being willing to die for us. Nothing else can begin to compare with the total surrender of self for the glory of

God as does this great act of love and obedience. We are told that he went as "a lamb to the slaughter," only with this difference: he knew what was coming. Animals led to the slaughter may have a dim premonition of their fate, but Jesus saw his clearly.

"Jesus took the twelve aside and told them, 'We are going up to Jerusalem, and everything that is written by the prophets about the Son of Man will be fulfilled. He will be handed over to the Gentiles. They will mock him, insult him, spit on him, flog him and kill him'" (Luke 18:31-32).

He indicated that his submission and commitment to this course came from his love, not for himself, but for us. He said there is no greater love than this.

"Greater love has no one than this, that he lay down his life for his friends" (John 15:13).

This was not an easy thing. It was a bitter cup. He sought to avoid it if possible, but his supreme values of pleasing his father and of being a blessing to others held him to the course, until man's cruelty had exacted its full price.

We are inclined to think such love, such selflessness, such absolute commitment is the ideal and is beyond actual human attainment. But it is to just this sort of commitment and love that we are called. It is the essence of holiness. We are to be like Jesus in a willingness to lose ourselves in the pursuit of his will and glory.

"Let this mind be in you which was also in Christ Jesus, who . . . being found in appearance as a man, humbled himself and became obedient to death . . . even death on a cross" (Phil. 2:6, 8 KJV).

"Be imitators of God, therefore as dearly loved children and live a life of love, just as Christ loved us and gave himself up for us as a fragrant offering and sacrifice to God" (Eph. 5:1).

Few will be called to actually die as martyrs, but all of us are called to have sacrificial love that forgets self to bless others.

Self-forgetful love is the hallmark of holiness. We are to have this same mindset as Jesus, a mindset that sought to show love and compassion to all he met.

The Death/Resurrection Simile

A prominent theme, both in the gospels and epistles, is that a person must die and then be brought into a new life. Obviously, this is not to be taken literally, but spiritually. We are to die to the old way and live to a new way. This death is to be self imposed, that is, it is a choice we make, an action we choose.

"Put to death, therefore, whatever belongs to your earthy nature: sexual immorality, impurity, lust, evil desires and greed" (Col. 3:5).

"Therefore, brothers, we have an obligation—but it is not to the sinful nature, to live according to it . . . but if by the Spirit you put to death the misdeeds of the body, you will live" (Rom. 8:12-13).

Jesus spoke both of death and new birth. "Jesus replied, 'The hour has come for the Son of Man to be glorified. I tell you the truth, unless a kernel of wheat falls to the ground and dies, it remains only a single seed. But if it dies, it produces many seeds. The man who loves his life will lose it, while the man who hates his life in this world will keep it for eternal life'" (John 12:23-25).

"Then Jesus said to his disciples, 'If anyone would come after me, he must deny himself and take up his cross and follow me. For whoever wants to save his life will lose it, but whoever loses his life for me will find it'" (Matt. 16:24-25).

Jesus is speaking about attitude and values here. He is saying that the person who seeks first his own rights and pleasures will lose out, but the one who has let them go for something better will win out in the end. He is speaking of a change in the mindset, a new set of goals and purposes in life. He says it is comparable to taking up the cross (an instrument of death), and a seed dying to germinate in the ground.

This death is not to be confused with our spiritual linkage with the death and resurrection of Christ. By believing in him, we are united with him in his death and resurrection for our forgiveness and justification. But this further simile of death and new life has to do with the commitment necessary for holiness. The first is a gracious act of God done for us in Christ. The second is an action we must take, by a deliberate choice, resulting in a new mindset. It is our full dedication which God consecrates.

Our Choice

These examples help us to see that a radical out-and-out commitment is called for of those who would live a holy life. Such a commitment is a matter of choice. Holy living is contingent upon having chosen the right mindset. If one is to live a holy life, it will only happen if his value system has been drastically altered. A holy life emanates from the will. To change the will is to change the behavior. So this matter of mindset is crucial. How do we go about making this choice?

It may be helpful to picture one's will as the throne-room of his life. Here, by nature, the desires for Pleasure, Possessions, and Position reign and dominate behavior. As long as this regime stays in power, behavior will be selfish and far from holy. What is needed is an overthrow of these ruling powers. By a deliberate choice, the will can reject and throw out this selfish value system and enthrone the values of Jesus. With his values (to Glorify God, to Do His Will, to Be a Blessing) on the throne and in command, behavior will begin to change and become more and more like that of Jesus.

The will can make this choice. This is the wonder of the free will God has given us. We can choose our own value system. We can choose whether we will live for self or for God. All poor human behavior comes from a will that is dominated by selfishness. All holy living emanates from a will that has chosen heavenly values.

For many years I was frustrated in my personal quest for a holy life because I mistakenly thought a change in my value system would come about by a special work of the Holy Spirit. I prayed and waited long for God to change my inner man. It was only after I realized that *I* had to be the agent of change, that it was up to *me* to change my value system, that holy living became possible. There is no doubt that the Holy Spirit led me to this point, and helped me make the change, but as a free moral agent, it was something I had to do.

This is one thing we can change quickly. It may take a while to work up to it, to get to the place where we want God's touch on our life more than anything else, but the actual change is done in a moment. It may be a crisis experience, a very hard choice to make, but it requires no long process. It is a matter of choosing, making a decision. Adopting as one's own the value system of Jesus starts one on the pathway to a holy life.

However, if one is to be holy, he can't vacillate back and forth between the godly and the selfish. The choice for God must be complete and irrevocable. It is as if one is sweeping clean the command center of his life. Jesus warned that if one does this and then vacillates, he will end up worse off than before. (See Matt. 12:45)

This act of the will, this choosing the values of Jesus Christ as our model, this setting of the mind to live to the glory of God, *we* can do and must do. Are we saved by grace but sanctified by works? Not at all! Both in salvation and sanctification there is a human response necessary for God's work to be done in us. In salvation it is to repent and believe. In sanctification it is to submit and sanctify ourselves. These responses are only possible by the grace of God. Even though it is an act that appears to spring from human volition, God the Holy Spirit is deeply involved. We can no more claim to have arrived at a willingness to fully commit all to God all by ourselves any more than we can claim to have arrived at faith and repentance by ourselves at salvation. It is all by the wonderful grace of God.

Let us look next at how the Holy Spirit is involved in our sanctification.

Discussion Starters:

1. What has been your experience at keeping New Years' resolutions? Why is it so hard?
2. Which of the four Biblical metaphors speaks to you the most about the scope of the change needed?

   Jesus willing to leave heaven
   Offering ourselves as a living sacrifice
   Jesus willing to go all the way to the cross
   The death of self/resurrection simile.

3. Do you agree that we have the freedom to choose the values that dominate our lives?
4. How is the Holy Spirit involved in our choosing of values?

Chapter 10

Unleashing the Holy Spirit

Of the three persons in the godhead (Father, Son, and Holy Spirit), the Holy Spirit is the most mysterious to us. We can picture God the Father, majestic and lifted up, on a glorious throne, governing the universe. We can picture God the Son, Jesus Christ our Savior, seated at his right hand, ever making intercession for us. But when it comes to having a clear image of the Holy Spirit and his actions, we tend to have only vague ideas.

Perhaps the clearest picture given of the Holy Spirit is that of the wind. It is invisible, but everywhere present. Every moment active, at times it moves great weather systems, and at other times gently caresses every little leaf. The Holy Spirit could be considered the active, immanent presence of God, working every minute, everywhere, and in everyone, to expedite the will and purposes of God. He is the great love of God reaching out to put into effect Redemption (Chapter 5). He is at work to bring all mankind both to salvation and to holiness. Man has no hope of living a holy life apart from the gracious guidance and empowerment of the Holy Spirit. Let us try to get a clearer picture of the Holy Spirit and how his power can be unleashed in our lives.

A picture of the Holy Spirit at work is suggested in the Old Testament account of Abraham selecting a wife for his son Isaac (Genesis 24). Abraham, living as a pilgrim in a foreign land, did not want his son to marry a local woman. So he sent his chief steward back to his relatives in his native land to find a wife for Isaac. It is a story of God miraculously guiding the steward to just the right home and the right girl, Rebekah. Lavish gifts were given, and Rebekah agreed to go. While the record does not tell anything of the long journey home, by the time it was over, the chief steward probably had filled her with stories of Isaac's beauty and character. When Rebecca and Isaac met, it was love at first sight.

The mission of the chief steward can be considered a reflection of the two-fold work of the Holy Spirit. He seeks and woos would-be candidates to be united to Jesus Christ, and when they have consented, guides and teaches them until they are ready to actually be married to him as the bride of Christ. This is the work of the Holy Spirit: leading people to salvation (prevenient grace), and leading people to holiness (sanctifying grace). Both are works of grace in that they are expressions of God's love and care, initiated by him, in spite of the fact that we are sinful and unworthy. Grace is God's unmerited favor.

Although it is our part to repent and believe in order to be saved, we are plainly told that the ability to do so is a gift of God.

"For it is by grace you have been saved, through faith - and this not from yourselves, it is the gift of God—not by works, so that no one can boast" (Eph. 2:8-9).

It is the Holy Spirit who brings to our mind the awareness and attitude we need in order to be saved.

"When He comes (the Holy Spirit), he will convict the world of guilt in regard to sin and righteousness and judgment" (John 16:8).

In the parable Jesus told of the prodigal son (Luke 16), the turning point in the life of this wayward child was when he "came to his senses." While the main message of this parable was to reveal the great love of God for those gone astray, the fact that Jesus mentioned this "coming to his senses" could well be a secondary lesson in this parable showing how the Holy Spirit works. Many prodigals never come to their senses, but here was one who received most undeservedly the gift of repentance. Even while living the most dissolute life, the ever-present Holy Spirit was protecting, convicting, shaping circumstances, and finally giving him the idea and will to repent. Each of us, who has been saved, can look back and see how the hand of God, the prevenient grace of God, was at work in our lives, often for many years, until we finally repented and trusted Jesus for our salvation. This is the Holy Spirit at work, leading us to the point of being willing to go with him.

In the same way, the Holy Spirit works in the life of the Christian to bring him to holiness. He seeks to reveal the beauty of Jesus, desiring that we come to know him better. His goal is that we not only be Christian in name, but that we become Christ-like in nature and deed. By his tutelage we see how unlike Christ we are when our chief desires are for Pleasure, Possessions, and Position. It is the Holy Spirit who brings us to turn from these things and to make a full commitment to the things of God. When a person comes to the place where he is willing to die out to these carnal desires, and put on the mind of Christ, the desire for God's Glory, God's Will, and to Be a Blessing, it is the result of the Holy Spirit at work in him. It is his sanctifying grace that leads to the willingness to adopt the mindset of Jesus.

We have attempted to show how the Holy Spirit has been active in our lives, both before and after our conversion. He seeks to move us from a spirit of rebellion and disobedience to a submissive spirit of obedience. But his role goes beyond this. He desires to bring the Spirit of Jesus fully into our hearts so that the power of his love will dominate us. Paul reveals this in his prayer for the Christians at Ephesus.

"I pray that out of his glorious riches he may strengthen you with power through his Spirit in your inner being; so that . . . rooted and established in love, (you) may have power together with all the saints to grasp how wide and long and high and deep is the love of Christ, and to know this love that surpasses knowledge, that you may be filled to the measure of all the fullness of God" (Eph. 3:17-19).

The Apostle Paul, writing to the "faithful saints in Christ Jesus" (1:1) who "have been saved by grace, through faith" (2:9), is urging them onward to a higher level of involvement with the Holy Spirit, a level where the Holy Spirit brings power in the inner man. He visualizes them deeply immersed in the love of Christ and "filled to the measure of the fullness of God" (3:19). The Holy Spirit would provide a new dynamic within for spiritual living, a dynamic not before present. You might say Paul prayed that the power of the Holy Spirit would be unleashed in their lives.

Reference to such an "unleashing" in no way implies that the Holy Spirit is not present in the life of every believer. Instead, it confirms that he is there, but limited in what he can do. At the moment of new birth the soul is regenerated by the Spirit who brings life where there had been death. He brings the witness of salvation with peace and assurance. But since the time for full surrender of self usually comes later, after a time of growth and testing, the full power of the Holy Spirit is constrained as our deep-seated selfish desires vie for supremacy. Paul was praying that they would come through this time of struggle into the full power of the Holy Spirit.

Jesus also referred to the receiving of power after the Holy Spirit had come.

"But you will receive power when the Holy Spirit comes on you, and you will be my witnesses" (Acts. 1:8).

What is this power? What form or expression does it take in our lives? Does it mean supernatural manifestations? Does it bring immediate victory over every character flaw? Does its presence mean the full end of doubt, depression, and fear? While with some it may work this way, this is not the norm. Extravagant claims and teachings in this area have led many to expect the wrong thing. How very important it is that we have a clear and correct concept of what the power of the Holy Spirit can mean in our lives. Setting aside the fact that there may be bells and whistles at the time we commit all and unleash this power, the residual impact of the power of the Holy Spirit in us is registered in the following ways:

- an increased desire to be true to Jesus, to have his love flow through us, to never leave him or give up in our Christian pilgrimage.
- a determination to do right, regardless how costly, with a deep faith that God will work things out eventually.
- a growing concern for others, a compassion beyond normal human love, that leads to helping others in some kind of ministry.
- the providential fulfillment of God's will and purposes in our life, being led on by him.
- a continuing spirit of obedience, praise, and hunger for the things of God.
- the development and living out of the fruit of the Spirit.

In other words, the power of the Holy Spirit in us is a divine reinforcement of the spiritual values, which to some degree, became ours at the time of our salvation. When we put on the spiritual values of Jesus, thus bringing our will into fill alignment with the holiness of God, the Holy Spirit is able to exert his *full* influence in us, since we now agree with him on what is important. The moment of full surrender and putting on the mindset of Christ is the moment the power of the Holy Spirit is unleashed in us.

The Holy Spirit is also called the "Spirit of Christ" (Romans 8:9), and we are correct if we assume that the Holy Spirit is the living presence of Christ in us. This being true, it is clear how the Holy Spirit can become a greater source of power when we have adopted the mindset of Christ. The elevation of Christ's values to a place of priority in our lives gives the Holy Spirit a new freedom to guide and infuse us with divine power. With the mindset of Christ, we are no longer in a relationship of reluctance or resistance to the Spirit, but in a relationship of cooperation, with both moving in the same direction.

This close relationship between the mindset and the power of the Holy Spirit in us is emphatically stated by the Apostle Paul.

"Those who live according to the sinful nature have their minds set on what that nature desires; but those who live in accordance with the Spirit have their minds set on what the Spirit desires. The mind of sinful man is . . . hostile to God. . . . You however, are controlled . . . by the Spirit if the Spirit of God lives in you" (Romans 8:5-9).

In adopting the mindset of Jesus, and having the power of the Holy Spirit unleashed in us, we have entered into the way to holiness of life. We have become holy in our heart of hearts, and the stage has been set for growth in holy living. The process of significant change is accelerated. Little may be different at first, but the combination of commitment and power bring gradual, if not spectacular, results.

In the next chapter, we will examine this growth process, which leads from a holy mindset to an increasingly holy life.

Discussion Starters:

1. How has the Holy Spirit been active in your life? Is he a well-known friend or a mysterious stranger?

2. What two goals does the Holy Spirit have as he works in us?
3. How does the Holy Spirit's work is us to lead us to holiness?
4. Why would the Holy Spirit have greater freedom (be unleashed) to work in us after we adopt the mind-set of Jesus?
5. What are some of the ways the Holy Spirit impacts the life of those filled with his power?
6. What significant act on our part unleashes the power of the Holy Spirit in our lives?

Chapter 11

The Process of Growth

What a monumental problem we face when we start trying to change from a self-centered, indulgent, greedy person to one who is holy, like Jesus. We need to face the fact that we are addicted to sin. Habits of a lifetime have a strangle hold on us. How naïve to think we will be able to slip into a new life-style over night! Even though the change of the mindset is done in a moment the working out of this new mindset is a life- long process. Holy in mind, we now want to become holy in living.

All attempts to live a holy life encounter deeply entrenched behavior patterns cherished to gratify the cravings of our carnal human nature. While the mindset may say I want to Glorify God, Do His Will, and Be a Blessing to Others, the body in which we live is still bent on lust, greed and pride.

"For the sinful nature desires what is contrary to the Spirit, and the Spirit what is contrary to the sinful nature. They are in conflict with each other" (Gal. 5:17).

This conflict, this inner tension between our high spiritual desires and our lower human drives, will be with us until death.

"I do not say for a moment that holiness shuts out the presence of indwelling sin. No, far from it. It is the greatest misery of a holy man that he carries about with him a 'body of death'; that the old man is clogging all his movements and as it were, trying to drag him back at every step he takes (Rom. 7:21). But it is the excellence of a holy man that he is not at peace with indwelling sin, as others are. He hates it, mourns over it, and longs to be free from its company." (J.C. Ryle)

We will never reach a point this side of heaven where our carnal desires will go away. Our inherent selfishness, the behavioral habits of a life time, and outright temptations from Satan himself, will all seek to dominate our current behavior. That is not to say, however, that they always prevail. They will seek to dominate us, and at times will break through in our behavior, but because of our new mindset and the empowerment of the Holy Spirit, they will become less and less domineering. The longer we hold to our Christ-like mindset, the more influence it will have on our behavior. The tension between the Spirit and the flesh will diminish as the flesh loses more and more of its hold upon us, and the desire for the things of God becomes more and more natural to us. This increasingly brings a life of victory, joy, and peace.

In theory it sounds so good. In reality, however, the process is subject to frequent failure. Consider a man floating downstream in a fast flowing river. He decides that he will try to swim upstream, go against the current. His first strokes will be weak. He is out of shape with few muscles for swimming. Although he has changed direction, the current is stronger and he continues to move the wrong direction. He is tempted to give up and just go with the flow, but he keeps trying. Eventually he matches the flow of the river and even begins to move upstream. The one, who has changed his mindset and decided to go against the current of his human nature, will experience the same sort of slow discouraging start.

For a time we may not like ourselves because we fail to live up to the values we have adopted. We wonder if we will ever learn to control our emotions, our tongue, our lusts. During these times, it is important to remember that we are God's holy children, blameless in his sight because our mindset is perfect. As long as we hold fast to our spiritual goals, keeping firmly committed to be like Jesus, we are pleasing to him, who looks on the intent of the heart more than our performance. At times we will feel we are failing, and suffer tearful anguish and frustration, but the only real failure would be if we changed our mindset and turned again to wanting the things of the flesh more than the things of the Spirit. Holding firm, seeking the Lord's continuing help, assures us of our ultimate deliverance from the failures that come from our ingrained lust, greed, and pride.

Dealing with these failures is where the power of the Holy Spirit and our Christ-like mindset go to work. First of all, they will not let us become comfortable with any type of unChrist-like behavior. The Holy Spirit will be faithful in leading us on, showing areas of need and working in us to reveal every "spot and wrinkle." He will show us what behavior is not acceptable.

"But among you there must not be even a hint of sexual immorality, or of any kind of impurity, or of greed, because these are improper for God's holy people. Nor should there be obscenity, foolish talk or coarse joking" (Eph. 5:3-4).

On the positive side, the Holy Spirit will show us the beauty of Jesus and lead us to seek and develop the fruit of the Spirit.

"But the fruit of the Spirit is love, joy, peace, patience, kindness, goodness, faithfulness, gentleness, and self control" (Gal. 5:22-23).

The Holy Spirit will not only show us our need, but will be a source of power within to help us change. Each incident will bring with it a strong feeling of remorse. Over and over again, our mental attitude will cause us to think, "That is not the sort of person I want to be. That sort of behavior is not legitimate for me. It is not proper for me as a child of God. I want to be like Jesus. I want to Glorify the Father, Do His Will, and Be a Blessing to Others."

This singleness of focus, this clearness of purpose, always fortified and empowered by the Holy Spirit, will exert a tremendous influence on behavior. It is not unlike an early technique used by cattle ranchers in the west. In the annual rounding up of cattle, there would occasionally be a belligerent steer that would be more bother than it was worth. Rather then spend an inordinate amount of time trying to herd it they would simply attach a mule to the steer with a short rope. The enraged steer would jerk and pull the mule trying to get away. But the mule had only one thing on its mind. It wanted to get back to the corral where there was food and water. Whenever there was any slack in the rope, it started in that direction. It might be jerked around, knocked down, and pulled in a direction it did not want to go, but whenever it could, it headed toward the corral. It might take a few days, or even a week, but sooner or later, the mule would show up at the corral with the steer meekly following behind. Such is the power of a clear and single mindset.

We, too, may be abused, knocked down, dragged off unwillingly by inner drives we have not yet mastered, but each time we must get up, brush ourselves off, and start out again in the direction we want to go. We hurt inwardly because instead of bringing Glory to the Father, we have caused him shame. Instead of being a Blessing to Others, we have hurt others, often the very ones we love. Instead of Doing God's Will, we feel like we have played into the hand of the enemy. We are hurt and humbled, but not separated from God. The Holy Spirit in us assures us that we are his children and gives us his encouragement and support. By his help we stick to our commitment and resolve to keep trying. And gradually we do better, gaining more and more victories as we go on.

It should be obvious that we are not speaking here of a casual commitment. Religious fads come and go. Some go from one fad to another. They may help for a while, but the little lasting good comes from them. But how different it is with the holy child of God who has truly died out to self and made a firm commitment to the high spiritual values of Jesus. He is armed with a purpose and power that makes growth in holiness a dynamic life-long quest, not just a passing fad. His mind is set. He has established priorities in his heart of hearts. And regardless of the slowness of progress, or devastating set-backs, he stays the course.

Such a powerful combination, the fortifying power of the Holy Spirit and the determined mindset, brings results. One tends to move in the direction he is facing. If the heart is set on the right things, they become a part of us. It is true that we usually get that for which we sincerely strive.

"And we, who . . . reflect the Lord's glory are being transformed into his likeness with ever-increasing glory, which comes from the Lord, who is the Spirit" (1 Cor. 3:18).

This road to living a holy life, though headed in the right direction and destined for victory, is filled with many rough spots. We slip and fall on the way. How are we to look at these lapses? Are they sin? How does God consider them? In the next chapter we shall try to answer these questions.

Discussion Starters:

1. Tell of ways you have grown spiritually in the last year.
2. Can we be perfect in the sight of God?
3. Do carnal desires ever go completely away?
4. Failure in behavior can be expected. What would be an even worse failure?

5. What should our mental attitude be toward our personal failures?
6. The Holy Spirit fortifies and empowers us. What is our role in growing and overcoming our carnal weaknesses?
7. In what ways does a change of our value system differ from putting on a WWJD bracelet?

Chapter 12

Holy in the Eyes of God

We probably will never appear to be holy in the eyes of our closest friends, and not even in our own eyes, but God sees us differently.

How he sees us is related to our mindset. Jesus repeatedly showed how his Father looked at the heart and motive more than at actions. In his Sermon on the Mount (Matthew 6), he repeatedly denounced those who did religious things only to be seen of men. Jesus said that the Father looked at the inner secret motives and when they were right, that pleased him.

This truth was revealed to Samuel when he was sent by God to select one of the sons of Jesse to be the next king of Israel.

"When they arrived, Samuel saw Eliab and thought, "Surely the LORD's anointed stands here before the LORD." But the LORD said to Samuel, "Do not consider his appearance or his height, for I have rejected him. The LORD does not look at the things people look at. People look at the outward appearance, but the LORD looks at the heart" (1 Sam. 16:6-7).

The many Psalms written by David reveal him to be one whose heart was right. His mindset and values were on the things of God. Even though his performance was not perfect, his intimate relationship with God shows how willing God is to accept and bless those whose *hearts* are right. David felt blameless in the eyes of God.

"For I have kept the ways of the LORD; I am not guilty of turning from my God. All his laws are before me; I have not turned away from his decrees. I have been blameless before him and have kept myself from sin" (Psalms 18:21-23).

God looks on us as his children and holds us dear, just as we do our own children. Two small boys, visiting their grandfather, thought to help him by weeding his garden. They made the mistake of pulling up many small plants he had set out just the day before. He praised the boys for their help and after they had gone, retrieved and replanted the sets. This act would have been viewed very differently if the boys had deliberately or carelessly damaged his garden! The intent of the heart made all the difference. If human hearts can look beyond the deed to the intent, then how much more, God!

This compassionate Father-like willingness, to see past the unintentional missteps of his children, is seen in the Old Testament.

"For as high as the heavens are above the earth, so great is his love for those who fear him; as far as the east is from the west, so far has he removed our transgressions from us. As a father has compassion on his children, so the LORD has compassion on those who fear him" (Psalms 103:11-13).

The compassion of the Lord here is not based on performance, but on "those who fear him." This shows how God sees us differently when the mind is set on loving and serving God.

But does God actually see us as *holy* when our mindset is on him? The apostle Paul uses the term "saint" to identify Christians. This word is the same word used for "holy" throughout the New Testament. It is also translated as "blameless." If the error-prone, immature believers in the early Corinthian church were called holy (saints), then we must conclude that God sees some imperfect people as holy.

That God should see us as holy is hard to accept. We are confronted constantly by the gap between our spiritual desires and our human performance. Biblical terms such as "holy people of God," "saints," "sanctified wholly," and "dead to sins," do not seem to match the reality of a life that, at best, is still marked with human selfishness. This discrepancy can be rationalized away with the reasoning that all of God's grace, that is ours in Christ, may not yet have been appropriated, or that we must ignore reality and "reckon" in our minds that we are dead to sin. But to the honest seeker, such rationalizations wear thin after a while and leave him with a sense of frustration, guilt, and anguish over his failures, and worst of all, discouragement in his quest for a holy life.

This is not right. Jesus promised his followers peace and rest, not anguish! He never intended that his followers should be troubled by a festering sore of guilt and failure over their human imperfections. We seem to have laid a heavier burden on ourselves than he intended. He said,

> "Come to me, all you who are weary and burdened and I will give you rest. Take my yoke upon you and learn from me, for I am gentle and humble in heart, and you will find rest for your souls. For my yoke is easy and my burden is light" (Matt. 11:28-30).
>
> "Peace I leave with you. My peace I give to you . . . Do not let your hearts be troubled" (John 14:27).
>
> "To rescue us from the hand of our enemies, and to enable us to serve him without fear in holiness and righteousness before him all our days" (Luke 1:73-75).

In order to find this peace and rest, it is very important that we understand how God views us in this endless struggle with the flesh. Are our lapses and failures sin? Should we feel condemned over them? This depends much on our definition of sin.

"Failure to measure up to the mark," is one definition of sin. On the basis of this definition, each failure to match the holiness of Christ is a sin. Some accept this as the "correct way to approach the discrepancy between intent and performance. "We sin every day," they say, "so daily we need to seek forgiveness for our sins." They seem to have no problem with the thought of holy people sinning regularly.

Another definition says sin is the "willful disobedience to God's revealed will." This definition takes into consideration the intent or motive of the person and implies that if an action or behavior is not malicious in intent, nor deliberate, or if it was done in innocence (not knowing it was wrong), it is not sin. Accepting this definition requires that one subscribe to the concept that through some miracle of grace we can be blameless in the eyes of God. Un-Christlike actions are considered blemishes, spots, or wrinkles, not sin.

The concept of being blameless in the eyes of God is central to human holiness and the peace Jesus promised. Job is presented as one who was blameless in the eyes of God, not because he was perfect in behavior, but perfect in intent. Jesus saw Nathaniel as a man who was blameless (no guile in him) not because he was perfect in behavior, but perfect in intent. It is clear that God looks at the heart and when it is right, he approves of that person, even though his behavior may at times be wanting. Key scripture verses focus on being blameless.

"May your whole spirit, soul, and body be kept blameless" (1 Thes. 5:23).

"For he chose us in him before the creation of the world to be holy and blameless in his sight" (Eph. 1:4).

"But I lead a blameless life; redeem me and be merciful to me" (Ps. 26:11).

"Keep your servant also from willful sins; may they not rule over me. Then I will be blameless, innocent of great transgression" (Psalms 19:13).

The Apostle Paul encouraged Timothy to appoint leaders in the church who were blameless, not perfect. (See 1 Tim. 3:10, KJV).

Understanding that God considers those of us whose hearts are right as blameless (innocent) puts a totally different slant on our moral failures. We do not anguish and feel hopelessly wretched because we fail. Instead, we have a godly sorrow and a desire to do better. We do *not* sin every day. We do not accept failure as inevitable. By living our lives and making our choices by the values of Jesus, we feel his acceptance and his peace within. We are blameless in his sight.

Regardless of what we call our imperfections in behavior, the obvious fact is that they do continue in the life of the child of God. *Our behavior is not immediately made perfect at the moment of our salvation.* While some may be so endowed at the time of their full commitment to Christ, for most of us, our behavior continues to be flawed in spite of both the deliverance inherent in the death and resurrection of Christ, and our own determined, disciplined, Holy Spirit empowered living. Victory over all imperfections is a present *goal*, and will be an ultimate *reality* when we are released from the body, but for the duration of our days on earth we will have those times when our natural carnal desires prevail. We will grieve over such times, and struggle to change. However, victory will become increasingly ours, and those times of failing become less frequent. Honesty demands that we recognize that perfection in behavior is beyond our reach.

Since perfect performance is beyond us, and our behavior will continue to be flawed, it stands to reason that God views these failings, not as sins marring our relationship with Him, but as part of the learning and growing process. Failures in behavior that spring from weakness and ignorance, *when the heart is right*, are certainly viewed differently by God than those that come from a heart that is in rebellion, seeking gratification in indulgence. While it is true that God does not condemn sin in the sinner and condone it in the saint the Bible refers to God considering His children "blameless" when they stumble. For this reason, the second definition of sin given above is the one that is most helpful as we consider God's call to be holy.

"The saint, by New Testament definition, is a person who has been set apart for Christ and who, by the power of Christ, is seeking to live a blameless life. Paul was reminding (his readers) that holiness of life, and an unmerited blamelessness before God, is the remarkable condition to which they have been called." (*Words of Life*, 8/98)

It is not hard to picture the Father-heart of God watching his child learning to walk. Does the human father chastise his stumbling babe for imperfections in walking? Does he take offense and disown the babe? Certainly not. With love and patience he provides encouragement and help until the child can walk. Even in the years of childhood and adolescence, when poor judgment results in bad behavior (although the parent is concerned and hurt), he does not reject his child. How much more must this be true of God?

But what if others are hurt by our misdeeds? We lose control and say or do things that cause pain or loss to others. Dare we assume that this is not sin? Can we expect God to hold us "blameless" when we leave a trail of injury and suffering behind? When others are hurt, those holy in heart will seek immediately to right the wrong. What a flagrant presumption on God's mercy and patience it would be to think that God overlooks such errant behavior. It must be obvious that repentance, seeking forgiveness, and making restitution are required on an ongoing basis even in the life of those wholly committed to the Lord.

So what is the scope of this "blamelessness" which God ascribes to his children? Does it cover both our mistakes (occasional lapses into selfishness) and our carnal outbreaks that hurt others? This blamelessness is based on the justification provided in the death and resurrection of Christ. His righteousness covers us to make us appear before God just as if we had not sinned. Hidden in this way in Christ, we have peace with God and an on-going forgiveness that covers all of our aberrations in behavior, whether we call them "mistakes" or "sins." When we are in Christ, we are blameless and he sees us as holy.

This "blamelessness," however, does have limitations. What about willful disobedience, when one goes on doing the wrong thing even though he knows it is wrong? The history of God's dealing with his people reveals him to be extremely patient, giving countless opportunities to his erring children to repent and change their ways. Ultimately, however, his patience was exhausted and he rejected those who had been his very own. It is folly to think that we can behave improperly with impunity. *Being blameless in the eyes of God cannot be seen as a license to live as we please.* Nor can it be used to excuse ourselves from dealing with the imperfections in our lives. If the concept of being blameless in the eyes of God brings a complacency or indifference to failures, then we are on very dangerous ground and have misunderstood the nature of our justification in Christ.

Indifference to imperfection is completely foreign to the person who has the mindset of Christ. This mindset, which says its chief desires are to Glorify God, Do His Will, and Be a Blessing to Others, will cause us to cringe over every flaw in behavior and earnestly seek to grow, learn, and change for the better. When we have this mindset, this type of attitude, God is pleased, and holds us blameless as we continue to grow and reflect this glory more and more. And if or when we do hurt others, repentance will be swift with forgiveness sought and restitution made.

When we understand that the discrepancies between our holy aspirations and our actual behavior are normal in our growth toward holiness, we can accept the declaration that we are holy in the eyes of God. He considers us blameless as long as we have the mindset of Christ and are in the process of growing in holiness. In the next chapter we shall look at some ways this concept plays out in actual life circumstances.

Discussion Starters:

1. Do you ever have a sense of guilt and frustration over you behavior failures? Why? Why not?
2. Give two definitions for sin. Which do you consider to be the right one?
3. How does the scriptural term "blameless" relate to living a holy life?
4. Do you agree: "Perfection in behavior is beyond our reach?"
5. What dangers lurk in believing we are blameless?
6. What will the response of a "blameless" person be when he discovers he has hurt others by his behavior?
7. When are we considered *holy* in the eyes of God?

Chapter 13

Perfecting Performance

As those who are fully committed to the mindset of Christ, we rejoice in the relationship we have with him. He is our Savior and Lord, our ideal. He is our inspiration, our song, our hope. His Spirit in us gives us power, and is producing the fruit of the Spirit in us. We know that we are his, and he is ours. We are holy and blameless in the sight of God, at peace with God as we seek to serve, grow and glorify him.

But this idyllic relationship needs to be translated into everyday living. As wonderful as any theory or theology may sound, proof of its worth is seen in how well it plays out in life. The test by which any teaching on holiness must be evaluated is: does it produce holy people? Do its devotees possess the hallmarks of Christ's love and beauty? In other words, it comes down to performance. Let's take a look at a few instances and see how the "mindset of Christ" approach works in the practical outliving of holiness.

The three broad human areas where we are weakest and where growth is much needed are those of lust, greed, and pride. Given originally to us by God as the necessary human desires for

Pleasure, Possessions, and Position (see Chapter 3), these desires dominate us because we have given them free expression in our lives for so long. Let us consider how adopting the mindset of Christ will work out in a sample from each area.

Lust

The desire for Pleasure is a major part of our lives. God has given so much to please us. The great variety of the tastes, smells, sights, sounds, and feelings that bring pleasure to us is staggering. God certainly is not anti-pleasure. He delights as we enjoy him and that which he has created for us. But when we begin to live for pleasure more than God, when we begin to live to gratify our carnal desires, seeking first to please ourselves instead of him, this desire becomes *lust.* It can have a hold on us which will affect our whole lives. It is seen in many different types of indulgence: sex, food, music, art, or sloth (laziness). How hard it is to break free. Ask those addicted to over-eating, smoking, pornography, gossip, gambling, immoral sex, or other pleasurable behavior patterns about changing. They will usually admit that they have tried many times and failed.

Now let us imagine how the newly chosen Christ-like mindset and the power of the Holy Spirit in a person would affect one of these problem areas. Since the sex drive is so strong and often a key problem, let's consider this area. Here is a young man named Steve. He has grown up in a culture where sex was continually exploited in the media. His mind has been corrupted by exposure to pornographic materials. He had a wild time in his teens when surging hormones and bad companions led to experiences that now not only haunt his memories, but also cause lust for more. This is the background that Steve brings into his quest for holiness. Now he daily renews his new mindset, to Glorify God, to Do His Will, and to Be a Blessing to Others. He tests his behavior against this standard and begins to see how some of his thoughts and actions do not glorify God. He recognizes that these things are now "illegitimate" for him as the holy child of God and he desires earnestly to change.

But change is not easy or immediate. While most lustful actions will be quickly curbed, Steve fights a terrible battle with his lustful thoughts. Such thoughts seem to bombard him constantly, especially when in mixed company. But now Steve is very unhappy for thinking this way. After each incident, he chastises himself; saying over and over again that this is not what he wants. He wants to be pure in thought, and to be a blessing to others. Perhaps Steve feels he is failing. He may have seasons of desperate prayer, just barely clinging to the hope that he can change. But he sticks to his mindset, holds fast to the values he sees in Jesus. The Holy Spirit helps by giving him guidance and power. Steve begins to discover things in his life that contribute to his problem. Suggestive movies, books, pictures, TV and music, all feed the lust. He realizes that he must avoid these things. Steve is led by the Holy Spirit into a ministry, and he finds that as he gets busy in ministry, trying to love and help others, he loses some of his obsession. Gradually it subsides. It may or may not ever totally go away, but Steve begins to reflect more and more the beauty of the one he seeks to emulate. Having the mindset of Christ and having his Spirit within have led Steve to reject lustful thoughts as illegitimate to him. Gradually he has gained a measure of freedom in this area.

Consider the process again. Steve saw his actions and thoughts as illegitimate for him as the holy child of God, when measured against the standard of the mindset of Jesus. He grieved deeply over each failure, but each time reaffirmed his goal to be like Jesus. He removed, as much as possible, those things contributing to the problem. He became active in loving and helping others. He persevered in spite of repeated failures. He kept his faith. At every juncture, he had the presence and power of the Holy Spirit to help. Victory was not sudden and dramatic, but came gradually. His holy mindset led to the change in his performance.

Gaining mastery over such deep-seated problems is seldom abrupt. While some may receive a sudden miraculous deliverance, most will not. I recall dealing with one young man who had been encouraged to "pray through" and "claim immediate victory." In spite of tearful and urgent sincerity, he could not find such deliverance. His deliverance came gradually as he stuck to his Christ-like mindset.

Greed

The desire to have and own things is another of God's wise gifts to us. It is an essential element in the survival of the race. To gather, to build, to own, are institutions upon which societies are built. Jesus did not find fault with the idea of building a house (Matthew 7:24). He did not find fault with a man gathering and having riches (Luke 12:19). He did not teach that material things are evil, but that how they were held and used mattered much. One early philosophy considered all material things as evil. This idea crept into the early church and still persists in some Christian circles.

A problem arises, however, when one begins to value material things higher than his love for God. When desires for the things of this world become greater than the desire to serve and glorify God, it is called *greed.* Greed can take on many forms. It can become an obsession to make money and to own expensive homes and toys. It can turn to coveting what others have. It can lead to stinginess and outright abuse of others. It can lead to theft and a life of crime. The Bible calls greed *idolatry*, which is the worship of things instead of God. Even after a person chooses to follow Christ, greed and selfishness will have a strong hold upon him and represent a very difficult area to change.

For our illustration in this area, let us consider Mark, a committed Christian. He was married with two children and was employed by a Fortune 500 Company. His immigrant Christian parents had done their best to give him some of the comforts they did not have as children. The acquiring of things was very important in their home. His parents helped him get a good education and steered him to a good job. Mark was intelligent and ambitious. He moved up the corporate ladder quickly, each step enhancing his economic status. Each promotion brought more demands upon his time and energy, leaving less time for family and church. Then an offer came of a major promotion and a chance to become a member of the executive team which would require even more of his time. The thought of more wealth appealed to human nature. Love for money and what it could bring, is a tempting offer. But Mark had a Christ-like mindset. He knew that foremost, he wanted to be like Jesus, and be a blessing. This mindset was for him the standard, the plumb line as it were, to evaluate the proper course of action. He realized that his family, his ministry at church, and his own devotional life were more important to him than money and things. For him it meant that he should reject the promotion in favor of doing, what to him, was God's will.

Many grow up in families where the "almighty dollar" reigns supreme. Becoming a Christian, turning from a materialistic lifestyle, and beginning to value the things of God highest are very difficult. For a greedy person to become a holy child of God he must go against a firmly established greedy value system. Overcoming greed will be as much a struggle as conquering lust. But here too, when the holy child of God fails and lapses into greed, he will grieve, and label such behavior as illegitimate. He will reaffirm his goals, and determine to overcome. With the help of the Spirit of Christ living in him, love will gradually prevail and greed will be less and less of a problem.

Pride

The appreciation of status and position is another of God's wonderful gifts to us. He created man with a sense of dignity, of worth. He was made in the image of God. He was made to walk and stand erect and given a status of lordship over the rest of creation. A sense of ambition was placed within man, a desire to achieve, to excel and to be like God. Man was given the ability to think, to reason and to create. His setting was one which would require hard work. To survive would require planning and effort, which would result in accomplishments designed to bring satisfaction and a sense of worth. Man would reflect the divine when he stepped back and saw what he had done was good. God wants man to take a measure of pride in who he is and what he accomplishes.

But how quickly this desire for status and position is corrupted. When this desire becomes a ruling passion, when ambition overrides all other values, when the desire to glorify self is greater than the desire to glorify God, this desire becomes the sin of *pride.* This sin is seen in jealousy, turf wars, marital problems, aggression, violence, and leads often to civil and political strife. Pride can become a monster within that drives a person to ruthless abuse of all who stand in his way.

Pride was a problem to Ruby. She grew up in a home where there was little praise and much criticism. It seemed to her that her father did not like her and favored her older sister. Regardless how hard she tried, she could not please him. She was jealous of her sister. As an adult she was driven by a desire to achieve, to prove her worth. Ruby started attending church, thinking it might give her some advantage in getting ahead. She learned of Jesus and in time turned her life over to him, becoming a Christian and church member. She came to the time in her life when she surrendered all to Jesus with a determination to live for the same values Jesus demonstrated.

Now some of the old desires began to interfere. She found herself feeling jealous if others in the church were getting more attention or approval. She felt hurt when others were asked to do things, given leadership positions and she was overlooked. These feelings, and at times outbursts of anger, also affected her job. But as she began to measure this attitude and behavior against her new value system, she saw how wrong it was. Jesus did not strive for status. His desire was to glorify the Father, not himself. Ruby began to grieve when these feelings of hurt pride would come, realizing that they were illegitimate for God's holy people. The Holy Spirit helped her to see how much better it was to trust God for her future and her position, and to leave things in his hands.

Gradually jealousy was overcome and a sweet trust came in its place. At times she may still feel slighted or overlooked, but now these feelings are quickly recognized for what they are and rejected. She says to herself; "This is not the kind of person I want to be. I want to be like Jesus and leave my life fully in His hands." Ruby now serves with a sweet temper and a deep inner peace, content to fill the smallest corner if that is where God leads.

With each of these people, Steve, Mark, and Ruby, it can be noted that a clear understanding of the mindset of Christ, and a commitment to live by it, coupled with a humble cooperation of the Holy Spirit within, initiated a process that helped them cope with and eventually overcome very significant behavioral problems. For them, this theory of holiness worked. They increasingly reflected the glory of God in holy living. They have not arrived in the sense of being perfect in performance, but their ongoing commitment to the values of Jesus assures that they will continue to change and grow. They are indeed, God's holy people.

A key to their growth was staying focused on their values and goals. In the next chapter we will look at the importance of daily renewal to this matter of keeping in focus.

Discussion Starters:

1. Have you ever seen a supposedly religious person who didn't live a holy life? Any examples?
2. What is the bottom line proof of the soundness of a theology on holy living?
3. Give some of the ways yielding to a desire for *pleasure* can be seen in those who let it dominate their lives.
4. Give some of the ways yielding to a desire for *possessions* can be seen in those who let it dominate their lives.
5. Give some of the ways yielding to a desire for *position* can be seen in those who let it dominate their lives.
6. How does having the mind-set of Jesus help overcome in each of these areas?

Chapter 14

Daily Renewal

Resolutions are easier made than kept. Promises made at the beginning of the year are soon forgotten. Regardless of one's sincerity and determination, without on-going reaffirmation of the resolution, it will soon pass and life will return to its old patterns. This is also true of the determination made at the time of full commitment to live by the values of Jesus. This new focus for living will is significant only as long as it is constantly renewed and reaffirmed. Daily renewal, however, will open the way for God's power to bring tremendous change.

The Apostle Paul associated such change with the renewal of the mind.

"Do not conform any longer to the pattern of this world, but be transformed by the renewing of your mind" (Romans 12:2).

Paul reminds us in this passage that transformation comes by our action, not God's. We are transformed by renewing of our minds, something *we* have to do. By such ongoing renewal we will cease to conform to this world and become more and more like Jesus.

Too long we have prayed and longed for the Holy Spirit to transform us. Sanctification has been thought to be a miraculous touch by the Spirit where he changes the polarity of our nature, from selfishness to love. This appears to have been the experience of some seekers, but not with many. While it is the Holy Spirit who leads us to the desire to be sanctified (set apart for his purposes), only we can do this setting apart. We sanctify (dedicate) ourselves just as Jesus did (John 17:19). Paul says this is how we perfect holiness.

"Since we have these promises, dear friends, let us purify ourselves from everything that contaminates body and spirit, perfecting holiness out of reverence for God" (2 Cor. 7:1).

God has a plan in which he has chosen and sanctified us (set us apart) for his purposes, but the fulfilling of that plan depends entirely on us committing ourselves to that plan.

The word "renewal" suggests repeated effort, not a one-time activity. How often do we need to do this renewing? Paul said it was a daily matter with him, when he said "I die daily" (1 Cor. 15:31). We need to renew our mindset as frequently as we feel we have strayed from it. This could be as often as every hour, or at the minimum at least once a day. Jesus also required daily renewal of those who would be his disciples when he said,

"If any man would be my disciple, he must deny himself and take us his cross *daily* and follow me" (Luke 9:23).

Paul indicated that this renewal happens by putting off the old ways and putting on the new.

"That ye put off concerning the former conversation the old man . . . and be *renewed* in the spirit of your mind; and that ye put on the new man, which after God is created in righteousness and true holiness" (Eph. 4:22-44 KJV).

Here, again, Paul indicates that the way to true holiness is dependent on our action and it has to do with the mind. He urges the Ephesian believers to make a radical change in their value system, putting off the old and putting on the new. This process is connected again to renewal. It is not a once in a lifetime event, but an ongoing action, a continuing renewal in the mind of the new value system, a Christ-like mindset.

Most sincere seekers after God will have found a way, a time, to have daily devotions. But in addition to devotional reading, meditation and prayer, the person who has adopted the mindset of Jesus needs daily to rehearse before God the values he has chosen for his own, to renew his mindset. At some point in his daily devotions he will remind both himself and God of his desires in a prayer something like this:

"Dear Father, I want today again to live with the Spirit of Jesus in me. Like him, my desires are to Glorify You, Do Your Will, and to Be a Blessing to Others. Help me today to live by these values."

Such a prayer, repeated every day, will keep the focus of one's life clear. Behavioral deviations will be immediately recognized for what they are, and corrections made. All desires for Pleasure, Possessions, and Position will be kept in their proper place, secondary to these spiritual desires. By repeatedly setting one's affections on things above, the person will be able to live by the Spirit.

"In order that the righteous requirements . . . be fully met in us, who do not live according to the sinful nature, but according to the Spirit" (Romans 8:4).

This daily time of renewal will also be a time to consider how one did the day before. Failures may call for repentance and a prayer something like this:

"Dear Lord, I am not pleased with the way I handled myself yesterday. Please forgive me. This is not the kind of person I want to be. I want to be like Jesus. I don't want to bring discredit or shame to your name. Please help me to be stronger today. Make me a blessing and use me to your glory today."

This type of a repeated, humble approach to God will provide opportunity for God the Holy Spirit to correct, instruct, and encourage us. He is seeking to bring the fullness of Jesus into our lives so that we should also be conformed to the image, or likeness, of his Son (Romans 8:29). He can be counted on to be present with encouragement and help when we call upon him in this type of praying. We will leave the place of prayer with renewed insight to our needs and fresh determination and power. Isaiah reminds us that this is where strength comes from.

"But they that wait upon the Lord shall renew their strength; they shall mount up with wings as eagles; they shall run, and not be weary, and they shall walk, and not faint" (Isaiah 40:31, KJV).

It is not difficult to conceive how such single-mindedness, clear and determined focus will bring results.

Persistence pays off. The Christ-like mindset, when renewed daily, will be a force within that will keep wearing away at poor performance, much like the elements gradually turn hard rock into fertile soil. Some results will come quickly. Others may be a long time coming, but the process is irresistible. We indeed become what we truly want to be.

As important as a Christ-like mindset is, the basis for our relationship with God will always be our faith in him. In the next chapter we will take a look at the role of faith in our spiritual journey.

Discussion Starters:

1. Do you have short prayer you pray every day, a personal prayer you say from habit? Please share it.
2. According to the Apostle Paul, what or who is it that transforms us?
3. Identify scripture verses that call for the renewal of the mind.
4. Identify scripture verses that indicate renewal should be daily.
5. How often, and over what duration should we renew our focus on the mindset of Jesus?
6. Do you agree with this statement: "We indeed become what we truly want to be?" Why? or Why not?

Chapter 15

Living By Faith

Religion is an emotional thing. Deep feelings are stirred as we worship and pray. God provides moments of spiritual ecstasy, bringing euphoria unmatched by any physical experience. At times it seems our hearts will burst with joy, love, and excitement. It is not hard to mistake these glorious moments as a sign of holiness achieved. At the times of such spiritual highs we feel holy; we feel all is finally right with God and our struggle for holiness has finally ended. We have arrived. We are now filled with the Holy Spirit.

But when these emotional highs wane, it is obvious that the struggle is not over. The old problems are still there. We may seek to recapture the euphoria of previous blessings, but it gets harder and harder to pump up sagging emotions. If we continue to equate holiness with thrilling moments of emotional highs, our efforts to reflect the holiness of Jesus will gradually diminish, since it is impossible to maintain emotions at such a level. Perhaps this is why one of the most significant revelations in the Bible is, "The just shall live by faith" (Hab. 2:4). A holy life is primarily a walk of faith. It is linked to a deep faith that determines to persevere in seeking godly goals, both in good times and bad.

This is not to belittle the important place emotions play in our walk with God. William Jewett Tucker, an early American preacher says in *The Church in Modern Society*:

> "We cannot remind ourselves too often or too urgently that the truths of Christianity were designed to be felt. Christianity is written in the language of the great emotions. It is the story of the forgiveness, compassion, patience and sacrificial love of God finding response in the gratitude, devotion, trust and sacrificial love of the human heart."

Thank God for the passion and love that are the hallmarks of Christianity. Who would want a religion devoid of feeling and emotion? But we have all seen how short-lived is a relationship with God that is chiefly emotional. Faith is the great stabilizer. Faith is trust, a deliberate placing of one's confidence and hope in God. Faith is commitment, a distinct offering (as a living sacrifice) of one's life to God. Faith is persistence, a deliberate sustained effort to live each day for him. It is faith that is the basis for a growing relationship with God. It is the environment of holiness. An ounce of faith is worth more than a pound of emotions.

The Apostle Paul, the most significant voice in the early church, was a man who had experienced unbelievable highs, hinting at once having been "caught up into the third heaven" (2 Cor. 12:2). He had an overwhelming epiphany with Jesus on the road to Damascus. He received the mystery of the gospel directly from God (Eph. 3:3). It is doubtful that any other person has had emotional highs of this magnitude. Yet Paul never emphasized emotions. In fact, he leaned the other way, stressing faith and reasoned thinking.

"I keep asking that God . . . may give you the Spirit of wisdom and revelation, so that you may know him better. I pray also that the eyes of your heart may be enlightened in order that you may know the hope to which he has called you, the riches of his glorious inheritance in the saints, and his incomparably great power for us who believe" (Eph. 1:17-19).

Jesus also warned that emotions alone would not be a sustainable basis for spiritual growth.

"Others, like seed sown on rocky places, hear the word and at once receive it with joy (emotion). But since they have no root (faith), they last only a short time" (Mark 4:16).

Emotional spiritual experiences are very convincing. They can sweep us off our feet and cause us to reject or ignore sound judgment. But without the roots of faith grasping the bedrock of God's promises, the effects of such experiences last only a short time. Faith holds to the promise that God "rewards those who earnestly seek Him" (Heb. 11:6). Even Samuel Logan Brengle, the icon of holiness in The Salvation Army, found that emotions could not sustain him. He said that he never doubted that he was sanctified; it was a real experience that could not be denied. But he indicated that there were many times he wondered if he had lost the experience, times of emotional depression. A relationship with God built only on supernatural visitations, signs and wonders is not likely to last. Feelings are a poor barometer for measuring our holiness.

The Christian walk, instead, is built on faith. It has as its inspiration the faithfulness and goodness of God. It perceives of God as holy, righteous, and just, and the one who "works out all things in conformity to the purpose of his will" (Eph. 1:11). Faith clings to God, trusting that he will make a way for his people. It trusts him to give grace for every struggle and eventually shower with his goodness and mercy. It is a confidence in God that leads one to say along with Job, "though he slay me, yet will

I hope in him" (Job 13:15). This sort of trust leads one to calmly walk with the Spirit, abiding in his unchanging love as suggested in Anna Waring's words,

> "In heavenly love abiding, No change my heart shall fear;
>
> And safe is such confiding, For nothing changes here.
>
> The storms may roar without me, My heart may low be laid;
>
> But God is round about me, And can I be dismayed."

Thank God for rare moments of divine encounter, when God stirs us to the very depths of our emotions. They become milestones in our lives. But they are rare moments. Life is mostly a day-by-day trusting, doing our best, without any high spiritual emotional affirmations. By his help and our own determination, we bring his sacred presence into those earthly moments, making them divine. Life is holy.

It is in the soil of such trust that holy living grows. With the mind set on being like Jesus, living by his ideals and values, and the heart set on trusting God, we place our fate and well-being in his hands. Life becomes an exciting pilgrimage. It is a journey with God. He guides and blesses. He flows through us to bless others. He works out his purposes in us and through us. And in the process, we continually grow to be more like him. His love, joy, patience, gentleness, purity, grows in us, and yes, our performance becomes increasingly holy.

Faith and trust may appear austere and joyless. To help us get a full picture of the holy life, we need to consider one more thing, the enjoyment God has planned for us as we walk this earthly path.

Discussion Starters:

1. Tell of a time when you had a spiritual high, when you felt the presence and power of God in a special way.
2. Why is living a holy life primarily a walk of faith?
3. Why did seed sown on rocky places last only a short time?
4. In what ways does faith help us live a holy life?
5. Complete this statement: "An ounce of faith is worth a pound of . . ."

Chapter 16

Time to Enjoy

Some paintings of Jesus show him laughing. His head is thrown back as he laughs uproariously. Can this possibly be an accurate portrayal of him? Was there room in his life for mirth? Did he have a sense of humor? Did he enjoy life?

Our study of how to live a holy life has been presented in somber tones. We have spoken about the need to be very serious in our intentions, deeply committed to the values of Jesus. We have looked closely at the serious side of his life, so much so that we may have portrayed Jesus in such a way that the thought of him laughing and enjoying life almost seems scandalous. We need to also give thought to his happy moments.

Jesus enjoyed life. The Jewish culture called for frequent feasts and celebrations. These would include times of rich fellowship with good food and drink. Jesus actually began his ministry at a wedding feast. His use of illustrations from nature indicates his enjoyment of birds, flowers, seeds, the wind, growing things, the sky (a weather predictor). On this basis, we should see that living by his values did not exclude enjoyment. He lived a full life, a joyful life, and, yes, at times he must have enjoyed a good laugh.

The subject of joy and living life to the full were in all of his teachings and must have been seen in his life. In fact, some of his critics accused him of not being serious enough. The fruit of the Spirit (joy included) permeated his life. His ability for quick repartee as he bantered with friends and questioners must have at times led to humor and much laughter. To Jesus, holiness did not exclude joyfulness.

Jesus indicated that one of the reasons he came to earth was to help us find a full, abundant life. He taught how putting God first brings fulfillment and joy.

"I have come that they may have life, and have it to the full" (John 10:10).

He also promised that if we seek first the kingdom of God, our physical needs would be met.

"But seek first his kingdom and his righteousness and all these things will be given to you as well" (Matt. 6:33).

Having the right desires puts us put us right up there with Solomon, who because he chose wisdom was given other abundant blessings as well.

"The Lord was pleased that Solomon had asked for this (wisdom). So God said to him, 'since you have asked for this and not for long life or wealth for yourself . . . I will give you what you have not asked for—both riches and honor'" (1 Kings 3:10-14).

Those living the holy life have found this to be true. Living by the mindset of Jesus brings super abundant blessings, joy and laughter!

This final chapter is a plea to take time to stop and smell the roses. It is a plea to relish the goodness of God. He has lavished his love upon us by surrounding us with beauty and blessings. He must be disappointed if we are so engrossed in growth and mission that we don't take time to simply enjoy life. He has given us a world with an infinite variety of sights, sounds, tastes, emotions, mysteries, and challenges. We honor him by enjoying him and his gifts. He has given us this wonderful world to enjoy even though we are engaged in a very serious business. We need to appreciate and enjoy the glories of God all about us.

One church, a few years ago, claimed a new spiritual phenomenon, the Holy Spirit baptism of laughter. Its adherents say that when the Holy Spirit came upon them they could not stop laughing. While we might question their interpretation of this phenomenon, we dare not rule out the place of laughter in the life of a holy person. It may not be always uproarious or uncontrollable, but it will be there. In fact, I am of the opinion that no one has as much good natured, happy, joyful fellowship as holy living people. Laughter is frequent and often uproarious!

Enjoyment of God and his gifts does not mean unrestricted pleasure seeking. Seeking our own pleasure ahead of God's will is one of the primary evils associated with the carnal human nature. The holy child of God does not live for pleasure. But neither does he see pleasure as inherently evil. A life lived to Glorify God, Do His Will, and to Be a Blessing to Others will be a life with much pleasure, tinged with joy, glory, and yes, laughter. We will be resisting the Spirit if we do not allow the joy of the Lord to be in us and flow through us.

This is not an appeal to try to produce a grit-your-teeth type of joy. Dark times come. Our own suffering or that of the oppressed will bring us distress and concern. The urgency of the King's business will at times place great stress upon us. At times it will not be appropriate or possible to enjoy. We, too, will have our Garden-of-Gethsemane times.

But this is an appeal to count your blessings and to look around and see the extent to which God prospered and blessed you. Taste and see the goodness of the Lord. The joy of the Lord is our strength. Take time to enjoy as you live a holy life.

We finish with one final call to holiness from the Word of God.

"It is God's will that you should be sanctified, that you should avoid sexual immorality; that each of you should learn to control his own body in a way that is holy and honorable . . . for God did not call us to be impure but to live a holy life" (1 Thess. 4:3-7).

Discussion Starters:

1. When was the last time you laughed so hard that you almost cried? Tell about it.
2. True or false? "Christians laugh more than the unsaved."
3. What indications are there that Jesus enjoyed life?
4. What indications are there that God wants us to enjoy life?
5. Will we be joyful at all times?
6. Is pleasure evil?

Study Guide

This study guide is provided to help leaders who may use this book as a Bible Study for a small group. It also may be used by the individual reader as a means for testing his own comprehension of the material presented.

Chapter 1

1. What thoughts come to your mind when you hear the word "holy?"

   Encourage all to share freely.

   It is an attribute of God

   It infers perfection, moral purity.

   It can refer to sacred objects

2. Discuss these scripture verses that also refer to the Holiness of God.

   "The Lord is righteous in all his ways and holy in all his works."

   —Psalms 145:17 (KJV)

   Here the word holy is applied to God, and all of his actions.

   "Ascribe to the LORD the glory due his name. Bring an offering and come before him; worship the LORD in the splendor of his holiness."

   —I Chronicles 16:29

Here the beauty and splendor of God's holiness are given as reason to worship him.

3. Which of these statements is more correct? Discuss why.

   God has holiness. God is holy.

   Encourage all to share freely. To say that God has holiness infers that holiness is a possession, some special gift, or a state of grace that could be lost. The Bible says that God *is* holy, not that he *has* holiness. This distinction guides the seeker to seek to *be* holy instead of trying to gain a special experience.

4. The word "holy" in the Old Testament often means "sacred" or "set apart." Are there instances where it also refers to moral *purity* (righteousness)?

   Note these verses:

   "He is the Rock, his works are perfect, and all his ways are just. A faithful God who does no wrong, upright and just is he."

   —Deuteronomy 32:4

   Here God's perfection is related to what he does, not his status.

   "The ways of the Lord are right; the righteous walk in them, but the rebellious stumble in them."

   —Hosea 14:9

   Right actions, right ways, or right living are the essence of holiness.

5. Why would belief in the holiness of God help a person's spiritual life?

   Recognizing that God is holy, and that we are created in his image, provides motivation and a goal for our seeking. It also keeps us from being satisfied with anything less than a holy life, bringing hunger and stimulation to our spiritual life.

6. Tell of any person you have known who has lived a quiet life of holiness. (Stimulate response)

   Many who would never claim to be holy, live and serve righteously and faithfully. It may be a mother, a Sunday School teacher, a nurse. They demonstrate that it is possible to live holy.

Chapter 2

1. If you had created man, would you have done anything different?

   Consider what affect it would have had if man had not been given freedom to choose, or if he had been made of non-perishable material, or if he did not have any of the basic instincts necessary to survival.

2. Were Adam and Eve holy before the fall?

   They were sinless and innocent, holy in the sense that they were set apart by God for his purposes, but not knowing how long they lived in the garden before the fall, we do not know the extent to which they may have been holy in their lifestyle before the fall.

3. In what ways were Adam and Eve made in God's image?

   They were made in his image in that they could think, communicate, plan, appreciate beauty, create, and choose. They were also like him in being sinless.

4. What *spiritual* instincts did Adam have?

   They had a worship instinct, an inner desire to obey, fear, and serve God.

5. What *physical* instincts did Adam have?

They had the physical instincts necessary for survival in the physical world. They were the desire for pleasure, possessions, and position.

6. In what sense are the natural physical drives of humankind amoral?

   These beautiful instincts were given for man's good and only became immoral or sinful when they were given precedence over his spiritual instincts. Adam and Eve lived in fellowship with God with these instincts before the fall, showing that the desires in themselves were not immoral. They were amoral, neither good nor bad.

Chapter 3

1. Discuss this statement: The selfish tendency to lust, greed and pride exists in all people.

   Ask for examples or acts that arise from each of these selfish tendencies. The temptations associated with lust. The temptations associated with greed. The temptations associated with pride.

2. In what ways were the temptations of Eve and Jesus similar?

   Each was tempted in the three different desires that are at the core of the human nature. These are the desire for pleasure, possessions, and position.

3. What are the three instincts (drives) dominant in the human nature?

   The drive for pleasure (gratification of physical desires, food, sex, rest, etc.).

   The drive for possessions (longing to own things, coveting, getting money and the latest gadgets and fashions).

The drive for position (a striving for status, recognition, fame, power, authority).

4. What sins do these three instincts turn into when given priority in our lives?

   The instinct for pleasure turns into lust. The instinct for possession turns into greed. The instinct for position turns into pride.

5. What different methods did God use to progressively reveal his plan of redemption?

   The plan was gradually revealed through his interaction with his people, Israel. Their patriarchs, leaders, prophets, song writers, and historical events together shed light on this plan. The revelation was completed in the teaching, life, death, and resurrection of Jesus.

6. Did God's eternal plan include provision for man to live a holy life during his physical existence? How so?

   His plan was to redeem man to be holy in his sight, and restore an intimate relationship with him. As his redeemed children, they were to reflect his holiness by living a holy life.

7. In what sense is life a pilgrimage?

   Those redeemed have started a journey toward heaven. They see themselves as citizens of another world, aliens here only passing through this world. They are prepared to suffer the hardships of the journey because of the hope and joy that is promised ahead.

8. What impact would "pilgrims" have on the world as they passed through this life?

   As representatives of the Lord they would show and spread his love and glory. They would enrich and instruct in this world as salt and light.

Chapter 4

1. Is selfishness a problem to you? Is it a "pulsating human drive?"

   Encourage all to share freely. It is amazing the degree to which selfishness tends to dominate every decision we make. Discuss how this is true in our daily habits and interactions with others. With many it is not just a tendency but a dominant ruling passion.

2. What two provisions were included in God's redemption plan?

   It provided a just settlement for our sin (forgiveness), and a way to begin living a holy life.

3. What is the ultimate goal of redemption?

   The ultimate goal was mankind restored so he would again reflect the image of God and live a life that would glorify God. The living of a holy life would bring joy, beauty, love, and hope to life.

4. What beliefs may cause one to minimize the importance of a moral life style?

   Easy forgiveness by repeated confession can take away the need to live morally. Even the belief in eternal security (once saved, always saved) can make one careless in regard to behavior. Religious ceremonies and rituals can also give a sense of having God's favor in spite of moral failures. The belief that we all sin everyday can be another cop out for not living a holy life.

5. In what way are we saved through the *life* of Jesus?

   Jesus' life is a pattern of how to live a holy life in a human body. His teachings, example, and value system contain the insight and power needed to live as He did.

Chapter 5

1. Can you identify the moment you were saved? Where? When?

   Not all can point to a specific moment but their faith and obedience are an indication of spiritual life. Allow each person to share his or her experience.

2. What is the "spiritual gestation" period? How long does it last?

   This is the period prior to salvation in which the Holy Spirit faithfully seeks to bring a person to repentance and faith. It is also called prevenient grace, since it shows God at work even though a person is in sin and does not deserve such help. This period goes on as long as the person remains unrepentant.

3. What is God's role in the new birth? Man's role?

   God's role is that of breathing life back into the soul that has been spiritually dead. This is called regeneration. It includes forgiveness, adoption, and justification. God's role also includes the time of conviction and the giving of the gift of faith and repentance that precede new birth.

   Man's role is to humble himself before God, to admit his sinful condition, to ask forgiveness, to commit himself to trying to live an obedient life by turning from all his sinful ways, and to place his confidence and hope in Jesus' death as payment-in-full for all his sins. Simply put, it is repentance and faith.

4. Describe the meaning of "repentance."

   Repentance means changing one's attitude from rebellion/disobedience to submission/obedience. It is a change of heart. It includes sorrow for sin, and a new strong desire to sin no more.

5. Describe the meaning of "faith."

   Faith means placing one's confidence in God. This faith is based on the promises and provisions revealed in the Bible. At the moment of new birth, it includes an awareness that one cannot get to heaven on his own merit, or good works, so instead faith is placed on the mercy and goodness of God who gave his son as a payment for sin. Faith says, "I believe Jesus died for me and because of this I can be saved."

6. Do all people who have been born again have a "miracle" moment when they experience new birth?

   No, there is no universal cookie-cutter process. Many have a dramatic moment of awakening followed by great peace, joy, and a euphoric witness of the Spirit. With some it comes very early in life. Some grow up in church but do not have their awakening until in mid-life.

   With some, the transition to faith and obedience has been gradual, without fanfare. They cannot recall a specific time when they were saved, but know it must have happened because their lives are lived in obedience and faith.

Chapter 6

1. Share about the greatest joy you ever had over a baby being born.

   Encourage all to share freely.

2. In what ways are the birth of a baby and being born again similar?

   Both follow a gestation period. Both produce a new life. Both are deemed a miracle. Both bring great joy. Both are just the very beginning of a life with great potential. Both need loving care to survive. Both need to learn to eat, talk, and walk. Both progress to maturity slowly.

3. What is the status with God of a newly born again Christian?

   The new convert has the status of being holy, a saint in the eyes of God. Since he belongs to God (by adoption) and is set apart by God (sanctified) for his purposes, he is considered God's holy child.

4. What is there in the human nature that powerfully resists efforts to change?

   Selfish habits and activities are like deep ruts that are hard to get out of. When change is attempted, one discovers that the human nature is basically selfish and exerts a relentless and unending yearning for self-gratification. The natural drives for pleasure, possessions, and position never go away. The new born begins a life-long battle to keep these drives properly constrained and subordinate to his higher goals.

5. Do you agree that many Christians settle for something less than living a holy life? Why is this so?

   Encourage discussion. The chief reason with many is that even though they have tried over and over again to master selfish drives, they have not been able to do it. It is an awareness of their own weakness and the compelling power of the carnal nature that seems to demand a realistic view that holy living is impossible.

6. Name some religious "cures" that have not produced the desired results.

   Some have sought a miraculous cure, the eradication of the carnal nature by the baptism of the Holy Spirit. Some believed the gift of tongues would signal a change in the human nature. Some have sought a baptism of love that would once and forever subdue selfish tendencies. Some have sought a second work of grace that would eradicate the carnal nature. Some have attempted severe self-discipline to master the carnal nature.

Chapter 7

1. Have you ever gotten lost? How did you find your way again?

   Encourage all to share freely.

2. How does Paul say we can get victory over our carnal nature? Does this make sense to you?

   He says that those who have their mind set on the things of the Spirit will not be condemned. This follows after he says that one can be rescued from the carnal nature through Jesus Christ. He does not claim that self-denial or perfection would deliver, but the spiritual mindset (of Christ).

3. Describe what is meant by "mindset."

   Our "mindset" is the values we have established as most important to us. It is the things that we by choice try to make the ruling desires in our lives. It is the focus of our goals and ambitions in life.

4. Do you agree with the statement: "Mindset determines destiny?"

   Encourage all to share freely.

5. Why did Job please God? In what sense was he perfect?

   Job was said to fear God and reject evil. Both of these qualities refer to his mindset. God considered him holy (perfect) because of this mindset. No mention is made of being flawless in his performance. It is as if God saw past any un-willful wrong behavior because his intent was always right.

6. When does God consider us *blameless*?

   The blamelessness God puts upon us is always based on the motives and intent behind our actions. If it were otherwise, we would never have peace because we can never achieve perfection in our performance. If we did not mean to hurt another by some errant word or deed, he does not place condemnation and guilt upon us, but overlooks it and considers us blameless because our action was not willful.

Chapter 8

1. Have you ever tried the WWJD plan? Did it work?

   The WWJD (what would Jesus do?) plan was introduced in the book, In His Steps by Sheldon Jones in 1975. It proposed that Christians should use this question as a guide for all of their decisions in life. It was helpful to many. Encourage all to share freely any experience they had trying this plan. Ask if they still use it and if not, why not.

2. Do scriptures encourage us to imitate Jesus' actions, or His mindset?

   Followers of Christ are encouraged to be like Jesus, to imitate him but the clearest indication is that we should be like him in our values, our mindset. How absurd we would consider copying him by being nailed to a cross. His actions give us insights into how to live, but it is in adopting his mindset that right actions result.

3. What indication is there in Luke 4 that Jesus had a human nature like ours?

   The temptations that came to Jesus in the wilderness at the beginning of his ministry were aimed at the three dominant drives of the human nature. The fact that temptations should be so directed is an indication that Jesus must have had a human nature like ours.

4. How did Jesus come to have a changed mindset? When?

   Although we cannot know for sure how or when Jesus adopted the higher set of values that became his mindset, we can assume that he must have worked them out in the give and take of childhood and youth. He seems to have made significant progress by the time he was 12 years old, as revealed by his encounter with the teachers at the temple.

5. What were the three ruling principles that guided Jesus' actions? Discuss the significance of each one.

   Jesus evidenced these principles as very important in his life.

   1) To glorify his Father,

   2) To do his Father's will by fulfilling his destiny, and

   3) To be a blessing, spreading love, teaching, healing, touching others.

   Encourage all to discuss how these principles affected his life and how they would affect their lives.

6. Discuss: "The correct mindset is the way to a holy life."

   Encourage all to share freely. Jesus obviously had his mind set on things of the Spirit and the result was that he lived a sinless life. Getting our act together mentally will always precede right actions. Without a firm commitment to the right value system, one will be led, not to a holy life, but a life marked by much inconsistency and failure.

Chapter 9

1. What has been your experience at keeping New Years' resolutions? Why is it so hard?

Encourage all to share freely. The difficulty in keeping such resolutions shows the extent to which our carnal nature dominates us and resists change. Trying to keep resolutions is also a matter of trying to change behavior, whereas the change needed is in one's value system.

2. Which of the four Biblical metaphors speaks to you the most about the scope of the change needed?

   Jesus willingness to leave heaven

   Offering ourselves as a living sacrifice

   Jesus willing to go all the way to the cross

   The death of self/resurrection simile.

   Encourage all to share freely.

   Jesus was willing to leave heaven. He willingly let go (did not grasp) his heavenly role to become a servant. We are to have the same attitude

   Become like a living sacrifice. This is the idea of the total sacrifice of self like a sacrificial animal. It infers the death or denial of self.

   Jesus submitted to abuse and crucifixion. Here we see love and self-denial to the extreme. We are called also to take up our cross daily.

   The death-before-life simile. A seed dies in order to grow. We save our life by losing it.

3. Do you agree that we have the freedom to choose the values that dominate our lives?

   Encourage all to share freely. Habits are very hard to change. But it is relatively easy to change goals and values. This is the basic area where our free will operates. We are free and enabled to choose what will be most important to us.

4. How is the Holy Spirit involved in our choosing of values?

The Holy Spirit is always at work in us to lead us to know right from wrong, and to develop a hunger in us for the right. When we get to the place where we are ready to die to self and take on the mindset of Jesus, we are only there because of the faithful encouragement and enlightenment given by the Holy Spirit.

Chapter 10

1. How has the Holy Spirit been active in your life? Is He a well-known friend or a mysterious stranger?

   Encourage all to share freely. Many may recall times of special "feelings" when a thrill or chill came. Some will speak of his help in prayer. Some may tell of how he led in a special way to help someone else. He also may have come during devotions, when reading the scriptures. These varied experiences highlight the activity of the Holy Spirit.

2. What two goals does the Holy Spirit have as He works in us?

   The Holy Spirit works to bring each person to salvation and to a holy life style like that of Jesus.

3. How does the Holy Spirit work is us to lead us to holiness?

   He holds up Jesus as our ideal and model. He creates a desire within us to be like Jesus. He convinces us of our need to reject lust, greed, and pride in favor of living with a mind set on the things of God. He helps develop the fruit of the Spirit in us, and enables us with his power in the inner man. He walks alongside us, guiding, upholding, and witnessing to our status in Christ.

4. Why would the Holy Spirit have greater freedom (be unleashed) to work in us after we adopt the mind-set of Jesus?

After we take the mindset of Jesus as our value system, we are on the same page as the Holy Spirit. Now it is a matter of pulling together, rather than against each other. With the spirit of obedience, submissiveness, and spiritual desires, we are open to his help and leading. Because our resistance is gone, it is like his power is unleashed in our lives.

5. What are some of the ways the Holy Spirit impacts the life of those filled with His power?

   We have a determined desire to be true and forever faithful. Our desire to do right becomes automatic. We care about others and are open to ministry opportunities. We have the grace to trust God to make all things work out, even when they go wrong. We have a spirit of thanksgiving, praise, and generosity. We desire the fruits of the Spirit and seek to have them grow in us.

6. What significant act on our part unleashes the power of the Holy Spirit in our lives?

   The act of rejecting the dominance of seeking for personal pleasure, possessions and position, and instead taking the mindset of Jesus, to glorify God, to do his will, and to be a blessing, is the critical action that unleashes the power of the Holy Spirit in our lives.

Chapter 11

1. Tell of ways you have grown spiritually in the last year.

   Encourage all to share freely. Are you handling tough situations better now than a year ago? Are you getting along with people (spouse, siblings, etc.) better now than a year ago? Are you finding it easier to lead and minister now?

2. Can we be perfect in the sight of God?

We cannot expect ever to be perfect in our behavior. But we can be perfect in our mindset. While we stick to mindset of Jesus, even when we fail in our performance, God holds as blameless and we are considered perfect in his sight.

3. Do carnal desires ever go completely away?

   The natural inclination of the flesh for pleasure, possessions, and power will never go away for they are what it means to be human. We may overcome and get lust, greed and pride out of our lives, but the natural desires will always be there and strive to gain dominance in our behavior.

4. Failure in behavior can be expected. What would be an even worse failure?

   The greater failure would be to give up and return to our old ways, rejecting the mindset of Jesus and no longer resisting the natural pull of the flesh.

5. What should our mental attitude be toward our personal failures?

   We should feel sorrow and be repentant. We should reaffirm our values and goals and reject these failures as illegitimate actions for God's holy child. We also need to recognize that failures are normal part of growth and not a sign of a lost relationship with God. We need to renew our determination to overcome and avoid the same failure in the future.

6. The Holy Spirit fortifies and empowers us. What is our role in growing and overcoming our carnal weaknesses?

   Our role is to keep our focus centered on the things of God. We need to daily renew our commitment. We need to keep close to God in prayer and reading of his word. Like Job, we need to "fear God and hate evil." We will move (grow) in the direction we are facing.

7. In what ways does a change of our value system differ from putting on a WWJD bracelet?

   A total overhaul of our value system is a much more profound change than a pledge to try to live like Jesus. One focuses on doing (behavior) and the other focuses on being (mindset). Trying to *do* what you think Jesus would do, is based on your knowledge of Jesus and his teachings, which may be limited or skewed. But having a mindset on his values will help understand more clearly the right actions to take in life.

Chapter 12

1. Do you ever have a sense of guilt and frustration over your behavior failures? Why? Why not?

   Encourage all to share freely. Guilt is universal even though some may seem to be free of it. It is as extensive as sin. Guilt is minimized when one knows he is forgiven, is sorry for his sin, and has a conscience that is void of offence (the right mindset).

2. Give two definitions for sin. Which do you consider to be the right one?

   One definition is that sin is a failure to measure up to the mark. It is to fall short of the glory of God. Another is that is the willful disobedience to God's revealed will. Encourage all to share freely their feelings as to which is right, and why they feel so.

3. How does the scriptural term "blameless" relate to living a holy life?

   The term "blameless" describes a relationship where one considers another to be guiltless, regardless of imperfections. To understand that God considers us blameless not only brings the peace of God into our lives, but also encourages us to keep doing our best. Without this understanding, frustration and guilt work against living a holy life.

4. Do you agree: "Perfection in behavior is beyond our reach?"

   Encourage all to share freely.

5. What dangers lurk in believing we are blameless?

   We may not feel the need to apologize and set things right when we hurt others. Some may think this blamelessness covers willful sin and disobedience. It may create indifference to failures and be used as a license to do as one pleases.

6. What will be the response of a "blameless" person when he discovers he has hurt others by his behavior?

   He will feel sorrow for the deed; have a spirit of repentance, a sincere desire not ever to do this sort of thing again. When appropriate he will apologize, seek forgiveness and make restitution. While he senses that God holds him blameless, he knows the person offended does not. He will make every effort to smooth out the offense.

7. When are we considered *holy* in the eyes of God?

   God sees us as holy saints when we have repented and accepted Christ as our Savior, and when he sees that the intentions of our hearts are set on the right things. He sees us through the righteousness of Christ, and as a result, holy.

Chapter 13

1. Have you ever seen a supposedly religious person who didn't live a holy life? Any examples?

   Many may come to mind, since it is so easy to see the imperfections in others. Care should be given not to get carried away in judging others. The main point here is to recognize that living right says more than what we profess.

2. What is the bottom line proof of the soundness of a theology on holy living?

   The confirming proof that one's theology regarding holiness is: *does it work?* Does it produce a holy life style where the fruit of the spirit is evident and the beauty of Jesus is seen? There is basically something inconsistent to well-developed theories if they do not produce the desired effect.

3. Give some of the ways yielding to a desire for *pleasure* can be seen in those who let it dominate their lives.

   Encourage all to share freely. Self-indulgent habits or addictions are a sign of yielding to the desire for pleasure. This can be in such things as pornography, gossip, gambling, immoral sex, sloth, etc.

4. Give some of the ways yielding to a desire for *possessions* can be seen in those who let it dominate their lives.

   Encourage all to share freely. The strong desire for money and the things it can buy, arise from this desire. It can take the form of stinginess, dishonesty, theft, coveting, trying to keep up with the Joneses.

5. Give some of the ways yielding to a desire for *position* can be seen in those who let it dominate their lives.

   Encourage all to share freely. The sin of pride is seen in jealousy, turf wars, marital problems, violence, and strife. It can become a monster within that can drive a person to be ruthless in his relationships.

6. How does having the mind-set of Jesus help overcome in each of these areas?

With a mindset on glorifying God, doing his will, and trying to be a blessing, these overt manifestations of self-seeking are recognized as wrong, as being illegitimate for God's holy person. With this awareness and the continued effort to live a holy life, these things are gradually overcome.

Chapter 14

1. Do you have short prayer you pray every day, a sort of personal prayer you say from habit? Please share it.

   Encourage all to share freely. Most will have short prayers said as grace before meals. Some will have a sort of "stock" prayer that they repeat often during the day.

2. According to the Apostle Paul, what or who is it that transforms us?

   Paul says that we are transformed by the renewal of our mind. This is an action that we take but God blesses.

3. Identify scripture verses that call for the renewal of the mind.

   Consider these verses: Romans 12:2, Ephesians 4:22-24.

4. Identify scripture verses that indicate renewal should be daily.

   Consider these verses: Cor. 15:31, Luke 9:23

5. How often, and over what duration should we renew our focus on the mindset of Jesus?

   This focus should be renewed as frequently as necessary, as often as every hour when we first start out, or at least once each day. After months or years it will become a sort of second nature to us and we will not need to repeat it as often.

6. Do you agree with this statement: "We indeed become what we truly want to be?" Why? or Why not?

Encourage all to share freely. This should be a time of sharing the faith and hope that we can and will change for the better if we keep our values right.

Chapter 15

1. Tell of a time when you had a spiritual high, when you felt the presence and power of God in a special way.

   Encourage all to share freely. These special times can come upon us anywhere, at church, at home, on the golf course, or at a sick bed. Think of the emotions the event brought.

2. Why is living a holy life primarily a walk of faith?

   Emotions are hard to sustain. They tend to fade. Emotional highs can seldom be replicated. When emotions subside, one's walk with God depends on his faith. Faith holds on and carries one through the tough times. It is the bedrock foundation upon which a holy life is built and sustained.

3. Why did seed sown on rocky places last only a short time?

   It did not have any root so dried up and died in the heat of the day. This is a reference to the need of sustenance that will support the exciting start. This sustenance is faith.

4. In what ways does faith help us live a holy life?

   Faith holds to the goodness and faithfulness of God. It provides stability during hard times as it believes God will work all things out well. This quality of hope and belief in the future helps us hold to our spiritual values and goals. In this atmosphere we grow, change and increasingly live a holy life.

5. Complete this statement: "An ounce of faith is worth a pound of . . ."

   An ounce of faith is worth more than a pound of emotions.

Chapter 16

1. When was the last time you laughed so hard that you almost cried? Tell about it.

   Encourage all to share freely.

2. True or false? "Christians laugh more than the unsaved."

   Encourage all to share freely. There are many joyful unsaved people just as there are many sour Christians. Joy is a gift of the spirit and it would seem that, across the board, Christians should laugh more.

3. What indications are there that Jesus enjoyed life?

   As a Jew, a normal part of the culture included festivals, song, and family celebrations. Jesus had normal human emotions; he cried at times and probably laughed at times, too. He spoke of rejoicing in several stories he told. His frequent use of illustrations from nature, indicate his appreciation of creation. His own reluctance to die would seem to indicate he valued life and the joys it afforded.

4. What indications are there that God wants us to enjoy life?

   He has given us a world of infinite variety designed for our pleasure and enjoyment. His Spirit is at work in the world to lead all away from the grief, guilt, and death to freedom, redemption, and abundant life.

5. Will we be joyful at all times?

   We will have dark times, times of suffering and distress, when it will not be appropriate or possible to feel much joy. We may go out weeping but will return later rejoicing, because of the Lord's help during these times.

6. Is pleasure evil?

Pleasure is only evil when we allow it to dominate our lives. The desire for pleasure can lead to lust. Pleasure, kept secondary to our higher priority values, is like the dew of heaven settling on our lives. God seems to bend over backward to please us!

Crest Books

Salvation Army National Publications

Crest Books, a division of The Salvation Army's National Publications department, was established in 1997 so contemporary Salvationist voices could be captured and bound in enduring form for future generations, to serve as witnesses to the continuing force and mission of the Army.

Shaw Clifton, *Never the Same Again: Encouragement for new and not–so–new Christians,* 1997

Compilation, *Christmas Through the Years: A War Cry Treasury*, 1997

William Francis, *Celebrate the Feasts of the Lord: The Christian Heritage of the Sacred Jewish Festivals*, 1998

Marlene Chase, *Pictures from the Word,* 1998

Joe Noland, *A Little Greatness*, 1998

Lyell M. Rader, *Romance & Dynamite: Essays on Science & the Nature of Faith*, 1998

Shaw Clifton, *Who Are These Salvationists? An Analysis for the 21st Century*, 1999

Compilation, *Easter Through the Years: A War Cry Treasury*, 1999

Terry Camsey, *Slightly Off Center! Growth Principles to Thaw Frozen Paradigms*, 2000

Philip Needham, *He Who Laughed First: Delighting in a Holy God*, (in collaboration with Beacon Hill Press, Kansas City), 2000

Henry Gariepy, ed., *A Salvationist Treasury: 365 Devotional Meditations from the Classics to the Contemporary*, 2000

Marlene Chase, *Our God Comes: And Will Not Be Silent*, 2001

A. Kenneth Wilson, *Fractured Parables: And Other Tales to Lighten the Heart and Quicken the Spirit*, 2001

Carroll Ferguson Hunt, *If Two Shall Agree* (in collaboration with Beacon Hill Press, Kansas City), 2001

John C. Izzard, *Pen of Flame: The Life and Poetry of Catherine Baird*, 2002

Henry Gariepy, *Andy Miller: A Legend and a Legacy*, 2002

Compilation, *A Word in Season: A Collection of Short Stories,* 2002

R. David Rightmire, S*anctified Sanity: The Life and Teaching of Samuel Logan Brengle*, 2003

Chick Yuill, *Leadership on the Axis of Change,* 2003

Compilation, *Living Portraits Speaking Still: A Collection of Bible Studies,* 2004

A. Kenneth Wilson, *The First Dysfunctional Family: A Modern Guide to the Book of Genesis,* 2004

Allen Satterlee, *Turning Points: How The Salvation Army Found a Different Path,* 2004

David Laeger, Shadow and Substance: *The Tabernacle of the Human Heart*, 2005

Check Yee, *Good Morning China,* 2005

Marlene Chase, *Beside Still Waters: Great Prayers of the Bible for Today*, 2005

Roger J. Green, *The Life & Ministry of William Booth* (in collaboration with Abingdon Press, Nashville), 2006

Norman H. Murdoch, *Soldiers of the Cross: Susie Swift and David Lamb*, 2006

Henry Gariepy, *Israel L. Gaither: Man with a Mission*, 2006

R.G. Moyles, ed., *I Knew William Booth,* 2007

John Larsson, *Saying Yes to Life*, 2007

Frank Duracher, *Smoky Mountain High,* 2007

R.G. Moyles, *Come Join Our Army*, 2008

Ken Elliott, *The Girl Who Invaded America: The Odyssey Of Eliza Shirley*, 2008

Ed Forster, *101 Everyday Sayings From the Bible*, 2008

Harry Williams, *An Army Needs An Ambulance Corps: A History of The Salvation Army's Medical Services,* 2009

Judith L. Brown and Christine Poff, eds., *No Longer Missing: Compelling True Stories from The Salvation Army's Missing Persons Ministry*, 2009.

Quotes of the Past & Present, A Compilation from the *War Cry,* 2009

Henry Gariepy and Stephen Court, *Hallmarks of The Salvation Army,* 2010

John Cheydleur and Ed Forster, eds., *Every Sober Day Is a Miracle*, 2010

R.G. Moyles, *William Booth in America: Six Visits 1886 - 1907*, 2010

Shaw Clifton, *Selected Writings, Vol. 1: 1974-1999 and Vol. 2:* 2000-2010, 2011

How I Met The Salvation Army, A Compilation from the War Cry, 2011

A. Kenneth Wilson, *It Seemed Like a Good Idea at the Time: Some of the Best and Worst Decisions in the Bible,* 2011

R.G. Moyles, *Farewell to the Founder,* 2012

Allen Satterlee, *Determined to Conquer: The History of The Salvation Army Caribbean Territory*, 2012

Helen Clifton, *From Her Heart*: *Selections from the Preaching and Teaching of Helen Clifton*, 2012